MONETISATION IN MOBILE GAMES

THEORY AND IMPLEMENTATION DEVELOPMENT

FIRST EDITION

Contents

Contents	1
Chapter 1: Introduction to Mobile Game Monetisation	10
1.1 Overview of Mobile Game Industry	10
1.2 History and Evolution of Monetisation in Games	11
1.3 Importance of Monetisation Strategies	12
1.4 Key Concepts in Monetisation	13
1.5 Purpose and Structure of the Book	15
Chapter 2: Theoretical Foundations of Monetisation	17
2.1 Economic Theories Relevant to Monetisation	17
2.2 Psychological Principles in Monetisation	18
2.3 Behavioural Economics and Player Spending	19
2.4 Game Theory in Monetisation Strategies	21
2.5 Ethics in Game Monetisation	22
Chapter 3: Monetisation Models and Strategies	25
3.1 Free-to-Play (F2P) Model	25
3.2 Premium and Freemium Models	26
3.3 Subscription Models	27
3.4 Hybrid Monetisation Models	29
3.5 Comparative Analysis of Monetisation Models	30
Chapter 4: In-Game Purchases and Virtual Goods	32
4.1 Types of In-Game Purchases	32
4.2 Virtual Goods: Definition and Importance	33
4.3 Pricing Strategies for Virtual Goods	34
4.4 Balancing In-Game Economy	36
4.5 Case Studies of Successful In-Game Purchase Strategies	37
Chapter 5: Advertising in Mobile Games	40
5.1: Types of In-Game Advertising	40
Banner Ads	40
Interstitial Ads	40
Rewarded Video Ads	40
Native Ads	40
Playable Ads	40
Offerwalls	40

Cross-Promotion	40
Sponsorships	41
Audio Ads	41
Social Media Ads	41
5.2: Integrating Ads Without Disrupting Gameplay	41
Contextual Placement	41
Rewarded Ads as Incentives	41
Frequency Capping	41
Customised Ad Experience	42
Native Advertising	42
Non-Interruptive Ad Formats	42
Transparent Communication	42
Balanced Ad-to-Content Ratio	42
User Testing and Feedback	42
Flexible Ad Settings	42
Dynamic Ad Insertion	42
5.3: Revenue Models for In-Game Advertising	43
Cost Per Impression (CPM)	43
Cost Per Click (CPC)	43
Cost Per Action (CPA)	43
Revenue Sharing	43
Subscription-Based Ad Removal	43
Rewarded Ad Revenue	43
In-App Purchases Combined with Ads	44
Sponsorship Deals	44
Programmatic Advertising	44
Direct Deals with Advertisers	44
Ad Mediation Platforms	44
Dynamic Pricing Models	44
5.4: Measuring Ad Effectiveness	44
Key Performance Indicators (KPIs)	45
Impressions	45
Click-Through Rate (CTR)	45
Conversion Rate	45
Revenue Per Impression (RPI)	45
Ad Viewability	45

Engagement Metrics	45
A/B Testing	45
Retention Impact	45
User Feedback	46
Return on Ad Spend (ROAS)	46
Analytics Tools	46
Heatmaps	46
Attribution Models	46
Continuous Monitoring	46
5.5: Challenges and Opportunities in Mobile Game Advertising	46
Challenge: Ad Fatigue	47
Opportunity: Personalised Ads	47
Challenge: Ad Blockers	47
Opportunity: Rewarded Ads	47
Challenge: Maintaining Game Balance	47
Opportunity: Cross-Promotion	47
Challenge: Regulatory Compliance	47
Opportunity: Sponsorships and Partnerships	47
Challenge: Measuring Ad Effectiveness	48
Opportunity: Emerging Ad Formats	48
Challenge: Player Retention	48
Opportunity: Programmatic Advertising	48
Challenge: Diverse Player Preferences	48
Opportunity: In-Game Events	48
Challenge: Technical Integration	48
Opportunity: Data-Driven Optimisation	48
Challenge: Maintaining Player Trust	49
Opportunity: Expanding Global Markets	49
Challenge: Ad Fraud	49
Opportunity: Continuous Innovation	49
Chapter 6: Player Retention and Engagement	50
6.1: Importance of Retention for Monetisation	50
Long-Term Revenue	50
Word-of-Mouth Promotion	50
Cost Efficiency	50
Enhancing Player Experience	50

Building a Community	50
Maximising Ad Revenue	50
Data-Driven Insights	51
Competitive Advantage	51
Predictable Revenue Streams	51
Reducing Churn	51
Leveraging In-Game Events	51
Personalised Experiences	51
Feedback Loop	51
Cross-Promotion Opportunities	51
Ethical Monetisation	52
Community-Driven Content	52
Maintaining Balance	52
Real-Time Analytics	52
Continuous Improvement	52
Monetisation Opportunities	52
6.2: Strategies for Increasing Player Retention	52
Onboarding Experience	52
Regular Updates and Content	53
Personalised Content	53
Reward Systems	53
Social Features	53
Gamification Techniques	53
Responsive Support	53
In-Game Events	53
Balancing Difficulty	53
Clear Progression Paths	54
Community Engagement	54
Cross-Promotion	54
Feedback Integration	54
Seamless UX	54
Monetisation Balance	54
Player Segmentation	54
In-Game Personalisation	54
Real-Time Analytics	55
Collaborative Play	55

Transparent Communication	55
6.3: Gamification and Engagement Techniques	**55**
Achievement Systems	55
Leaderboards	55
Daily Challenges	55
Quests and Missions	56
Progress Bars	56
Customisation Options	56
Social Sharing	56
In-Game Events	56
Virtual Economies	56
Feedback Systems	56
Time-Limited Rewards	56
Collaborative Play	57
Narrative Elements	57
Interactive Tutorials	57
Adaptive Difficulty	57
Rewards for Loyalty	57
Dynamic Content	57
Mini-Games	57
Interactive Elements	57
In-Game Analytics	57
6.4: Community Building and Social Features	**58**
Social Interactions	58
Multiplayer Modes	58
Guilds and Clans	58
Community Events	58
User-Generated Content	58
Social Media Integration	58
Leaderboards and Rankings	59
Community Forums	59
Developer Interaction	59
In-Game Avatars and Profiles	59
Collaborative Challenges	59
Virtual Events and Celebrations	59
Player Recognition	59

In-Game Surveys and Polls	59
Mentorship Programs	60
Community Guidelines	60
Cross-Platform Play	60
Feedback Loops	60
In-Game Community Spaces	60
6.5: Analysing Retention Metrics	60
Key Retention Metrics	60
Cohort Analysis	60
Churn Rate	61
Lifetime Value (LTV)	61
Session Length	61
Session Frequency	61
Active Users	61
Stickiness Ratio	61
In-Game Events Participation	61
Time to First Purchase	61
Player Feedback	62
A/B Testing	62
Heatmaps	62
Funnel Analysis	62
Social Engagement	62
Player Segmentation	62
Real-Time Analytics	62
Retention Curves	62
Benchmarking	62
Predictive Analytics	63
Continuous Monitoring	63
Chapter 7: Designing Monetisation-Friendly Game Mechanics	64
7.1 Game Design Principles for Monetisation	64
7.2 Balancing Fun and Profit	65
7.3 Reward Systems and Player Motivation	66
7.4 Integrating Monetisation into Game Narrative	67
7.5 Testing and Iterating Monetisation Mechanics	68
Chapter 8: User Experience and Monetisation	70
8.1 Understanding Player Personas	70

    8.2 UX Design Principles for Monetisation — 71
    8.3 Ensuring a Seamless Purchase Experience — 72
    8.4 Feedback and Adaptation from User Data — 73
    8.5 Avoiding Common UX Pitfalls in Monetisation — 74

Chapter 9: Data Analytics and Monetisation — 76
    9.1 Role of Data in Monetisation — 76
    9.2 Key Metrics for Monetisation Analysis — 77
    9.3 Tools and Technologies for Data Analytics — 78
    9.4 Interpreting and Acting on Data Insights — 80
    9.5 Case Studies of Data-Driven Monetisation Strategies — 82

Chapter 10: Legal and Regulatory Considerations — 84
    10.1 Legal Framework for Mobile Game Monetisation — 84
    10.2 Regulatory Issues in Different Regions — 86
    10.3 Protecting Player Privacy and Data — 88
    10.4 Complying with Consumer Protection Laws — 90
    10.5 Navigating Legal Challenges in Monetisation — 91

Chapter 11: Global Perspectives on Monetisation — 94
    11.1 Monetisation Trends in Different Markets — 94
    11.2 Cultural Differences in Player Spending — 94
    11.3 Localisation of Monetisation Strategies — 95
    11.4 Success Stories from Various Regions — 96
    11.5 Adapting to Global Market Changes — 97

Chapter 12: Monetisation in Emerging Technologies — 99
    12.1 Monetisation in AR and VR Games — 99
    12.2 Blockchain and Cryptocurrency in Gaming — 100
    12.3 The Future of Monetisation with AI — 100
    12.4 Monetising Cross-Platform Play — 101
    12.5 Innovations in Mobile Game Monetisation — 102

Chapter 13: Marketing and Monetisation — 105
    13.1 Marketing Strategies for Monetised Games — 105
    13.2 Leveraging Social Media for Monetisation — 106
    13.3 Influencer and Affiliate Marketing — 108
    13.4 Launch and Post-Launch Marketing — 110
    13.5 Measuring Marketing Effectiveness — 112

Chapter 14: Case Studies of Successful Mobile Games — 115
    14.1 Analysis of Top-Grossing Mobile Games — 115

14.2 Lessons from Successful Monetisation Strategies	117
14.3 Failures and What They Teach Us	119
14.4 Evolution of Monetisation in Iconic Games	121
14.5 Future Trends Predicted by Case Studies	122
Chapter 15: Player Feedback and Community Management	**125**
15.1 Importance of Player Feedback in Monetisation	125
15.2 Collecting and Analysing Feedback	126
15.3 Engaging with the Player Community	127
15.4 Incorporating Feedback into Game Development	128
15.5 Building Long-Term Player Loyalty	130
Chapter 16: Indie Developers and Monetisation	**132**
16.1 Monetisation Challenges for Indie Developers	132
16.2 Effective Strategies for Indies	133
16.3 Funding and Financial Planning	134
16.4 Marketing and Monetisation for Indies	136
16.5 Success Stories of Indie Game Monetisation	137
Chapter 17: Future of Mobile Game Monetisation	**140**
17.1 Predicting Market Trends	140
17.2 Potential Disruptors in the Industry	141
17.3 Evolving Player Expectations	142
17.4 Technological Advances and Monetisation	143
17.5 Long-Term Sustainability of Current Models	145
Chapter 18: Tools and Resources for Developers	**147**
18.1 Monetisation Platforms and Tools	147
18.2 Analytics and Data Management Tools	148
18.3 Best Practices and Guidelines	149
18.4 Resources for Continuous Learning	151
18.5 Community and Networking Opportunities	152
Chapter 19: Building a Monetisation Strategy	**154**
19.1 Steps to Develop a Monetisation Plan	154
19.2 Identifying Target Audience and Goals	155
19.3 Creating a Sustainable Monetisation Model	155
19.4 Implementing and Testing Strategies	157
19.5 Reviewing and Adapting the Strategy	158
Chapter 20: Conclusion and Future Directions	**160**
20.1 Recap of Key Points	160

20.2 Reflection on the Evolution of Monetisation	161
20.3 Challenges and Opportunities Ahead	162
Challenges	162
Opportunities	163
20.4 Final Thoughts on Ethical Monetisation	164
20.5 Call to Action for Game Developers	165

Chapter 1: Introduction to Mobile Game Monetisation

1.1 Overview of Mobile Game Industry

The mobile game industry has experienced unprecedented growth over the past decade, driven by advancements in technology, increased smartphone penetration, and the proliferation of app stores. Today, mobile games represent a significant portion of the global gaming market, with revenues surpassing those of traditional console and PC games.

The accessibility of mobile devices has democratized gaming, allowing people from diverse demographics and geographies to engage in gaming. This shift has broadened the market, creating opportunities for developers to tap into a vast audience. Mobile games are no longer limited to casual gamers; they encompass a wide range of genres, attracting both hardcore gamers and casual players.

Monetisation in mobile games has evolved significantly, moving from simple paid downloads to complex systems involving in-app purchases, advertisements, and subscription models. These monetisation strategies are designed to maximize revenue while enhancing player experience and engagement.

The success of mobile games like "Candy Crush Saga," "Clash of Clans," and "Pokémon GO" demonstrates the potential profitability of well-executed monetisation strategies. These games have generated billions of dollars in revenue, primarily through in-app purchases and advertising.

Despite the lucrative opportunities, the mobile game industry is highly competitive. Thousands of new games are released every month, making it challenging for developers to attract and retain players. Effective monetisation strategies are crucial for standing out in this crowded market.

Developers must balance monetisation with user experience, ensuring that in-game purchases and advertisements do not disrupt gameplay. This balance is essential for maintaining player satisfaction and long-term engagement.

The mobile game industry is also characterized by rapid technological advancements. Innovations such as augmented reality (AR), virtual reality (VR), and 5G connectivity are transforming the gaming experience, opening new avenues for monetisation.

As the industry continues to evolve, understanding the dynamics of mobile game monetisation becomes increasingly important. This chapter aims to provide a comprehensive overview of the mobile game industry, highlighting key trends, challenges, and opportunities in monetisation.

The subsequent sections will delve deeper into the history and evolution of game monetisation, the importance of effective strategies, and the key concepts that underpin successful monetisation in mobile games.

In summary, the mobile game industry offers vast opportunities for developers willing to innovate and adapt to changing market conditions. Effective monetisation strategies are essential for capitalizing on these opportunities and achieving long-term success in this dynamic and rapidly growing market.

1.2 History and Evolution of Monetisation in Games

The history of game monetisation dates back to the early days of arcade games in the 1970s and 1980s. During this period, monetisation was straightforward: players paid to play. Arcade games required a coin for each session, providing a clear and direct revenue stream for game developers and arcade owners.

As technology advanced, the gaming industry transitioned to home consoles and personal computers. The monetisation model shifted from pay-per-play to a purchase model, where players bought physical copies of games. This model dominated the market through the 1990s and early 2000s, with blockbuster titles generating significant revenue through sales.

The rise of the internet and digital distribution in the early 2000s brought about a new era in game monetisation. Digital downloads and online multiplayer games introduced subscription models and downloadable content (DLC). Games like "World of Warcraft" popularized the subscription model, where players paid a monthly fee for continued access to the game.

The advent of smartphones and app stores in the late 2000s revolutionized game monetisation once again. The freemium model, where games are free to download but generate revenue through in-app purchases, became the dominant monetisation strategy for mobile games. "Angry Birds" and "Candy Crush Saga" were among the early successes of this model.

In-app purchases allow players to buy virtual goods, such as power-ups, skins, and currency, enhancing their gameplay experience. This model leverages the psychology of instant gratification and incremental spending, often leading to higher lifetime value per user compared to traditional purchase models.

Advertising also emerged as a significant revenue stream for mobile games. Developers integrated various types of ads, such as banner ads, interstitial ads, and rewarded videos, to monetize their user base without relying solely on in-app purchases. Games like "Clash of Clans" effectively combined in-app purchases with advertising to maximize revenue.

The evolution of monetisation strategies has not been without controversy. The introduction of loot boxes and other gambling-like mechanics has raised ethical concerns and led to regulatory scrutiny. Critics argue that these mechanics can exploit vulnerable players and encourage addictive behavior.

In response to these concerns, some developers have adopted more transparent and player-friendly monetisation practices. The industry is gradually moving towards models that prioritize player satisfaction and long-term engagement over short-term profits.

The rise of live service games, or "games as a service" (GaaS), represents the latest evolution in game monetisation. These games, such as "Fortnite" and "Apex Legends," offer ongoing content updates and events, keeping players engaged and encouraging continuous spending.

Looking ahead, emerging technologies like AR, VR, and blockchain are expected to further transform game monetisation. AR and VR can create immersive experiences that open new possibilities for virtual goods and interactive ads. Blockchain technology introduces concepts like true ownership of digital assets, potentially revolutionizing virtual economies.

In conclusion, the history of game monetisation is a story of continuous innovation and adaptation. From coin-operated arcade machines to complex freemium models, the industry has evolved to meet changing player preferences and technological advancements. Understanding this evolution is crucial for developing effective monetisation strategies in today's competitive market.

1.3 Importance of Monetisation Strategies

Monetisation strategies are critical for the success of mobile games, as they directly impact a game's profitability and sustainability. A well-designed monetisation strategy not only maximizes revenue but also enhances player experience and engagement.

Effective monetisation strategies enable developers to generate revenue without compromising the quality of the game. This balance is essential for maintaining player satisfaction and ensuring long-term engagement. Games that excessively push in-app purchases or ads can frustrate players, leading to negative reviews and high churn rates.

Revenue generated from effective monetisation can be reinvested into the game, funding updates, new content, and marketing efforts. This continuous improvement cycle helps retain existing players and attract new ones, creating a sustainable growth model.

Monetisation strategies also play a crucial role in user acquisition. Free-to-play games with compelling monetisation models can attract a larger player base compared to paid games. By lowering the barrier to entry, developers can reach a broader audience and capitalize on the "long tail" of player spending.

Different monetisation strategies can appeal to different player segments. For example, some players may prefer spending on in-app purchases to enhance their gameplay experience, while others may be more receptive to watching ads for rewards. Understanding player preferences and behaviors is key to designing effective monetisation strategies.

Data analytics is a powerful tool for optimizing monetisation strategies. By analyzing player data, developers can identify spending patterns, preferences, and pain points. This information can inform the design of in-app purchases, ad placements, and pricing strategies, ultimately improving revenue performance.

Ethical considerations are increasingly important in monetisation strategies. Players are becoming more aware of manipulative practices and are demanding transparency and fairness. Developers who prioritize ethical monetisation practices can build trust and loyalty among their player base.

The competitive nature of the mobile game industry makes it essential to innovate in monetisation strategies continually. Staying ahead of trends and adopting new technologies can provide a competitive edge. For example, integrating augmented reality features or leveraging blockchain for virtual goods can differentiate a game and attract tech-savvy players.

Monetisation strategies are not one-size-fits-all; they must be tailored to the specific game and its audience. A strategy that works for a casual puzzle game may not be suitable for a hardcore RPG. Developers must experiment, test, and iterate to find the optimal monetisation approach for their game.

Cross-promotion and partnerships can enhance monetisation efforts. Collaborating with other games or brands can introduce new revenue streams and expand a game's reach. For instance, limited-time crossover events or branded virtual goods can create excitement and drive sales.

Regulatory compliance is another critical aspect of monetisation strategies. Developers must navigate various legal frameworks and ensure their monetisation practices adhere to regional laws and guidelines. This is especially important for games targeting a global audience, as regulations can vary significantly between countries.

In conclusion, monetisation strategies are a cornerstone of mobile game development. They influence a game's financial success, player satisfaction, and long-term viability. By understanding and implementing effective monetisation strategies, developers can create games that are not only profitable but also enjoyable and sustainable.

1.4 Key Concepts in Monetisation

Understanding key concepts in monetisation is essential for developing effective strategies. These concepts form the foundation of monetisation models and practices in the mobile game industry.

Lifetime Value (LTV): LTV represents the total revenue a player generates over their entire relationship with a game. Maximizing LTV involves strategies to increase player retention, engagement, and spending. High LTV indicates a successful monetisation strategy and a loyal player base.

Average Revenue Per User (ARPU): ARPU measures the average revenue generated per user over a specific period. It helps developers assess the effectiveness of their monetisation strategies and compare performance across different games or segments.

Increasing ARPU can be achieved through optimizing in-app purchases, ads, and other revenue streams.

Conversion Rate: The conversion rate is the percentage of players who make a purchase or engage with monetised features. A high conversion rate indicates that the monetisation strategies are effectively encouraging players to spend. Techniques like offering enticing starter packs or limited-time offers can boost conversion rates.

Churn Rate: Churn rate refers to the percentage of players who stop playing the game over a specific period. Reducing churn is crucial for sustaining a healthy player base and maximizing LTV. Strategies to reduce churn include improving game content, enhancing player engagement, and addressing pain points promptly.

In-App Purchases (IAP): IAPs are the primary revenue source for many free-to-play games. They can include consumables (e.g., power-ups), non-consumables (e.g., character skins), and subscriptions. Designing appealing and valuable IAPs is key to driving player spending.

Virtual Goods: Virtual goods are digital items that players can purchase and use within the game. They can be purely cosmetic, enhancing the visual experience, or functional, providing gameplay advantages. Pricing and scarcity of virtual goods can significantly impact player spending behavior.

Freemium Model: The freemium model offers the game for free while monetising through IAPs and ads. It lowers the barrier to entry, attracting a large player base. The challenge is to balance the free experience with monetisation opportunities without alienating non-paying players.

Ad Monetisation: Ad monetisation involves integrating ads into the game to generate revenue. Types of ads include banner ads, interstitial ads, and rewarded videos. Rewarded videos, where players receive in-game rewards for watching ads, are particularly popular due to their non-intrusive nature.

Subscription Models: Subscription models offer players recurring access to exclusive content, features, or currency for a regular fee. This model provides a steady revenue stream and can enhance player retention by continually delivering value.

Gamification: Gamification incorporates game-like elements into non-game contexts to boost engagement and retention. In monetisation, gamification can include reward systems, leaderboards, and challenges that encourage players to spend more time and money in the game.

A/B Testing: A/B testing involves comparing two versions of a feature to determine which performs better. It is a powerful tool for optimizing monetisation strategies. Developers can test different pricing, offers, and ad placements to identify the most effective approach.

User Segmentation: Segmenting players based on their behavior, preferences, and spending patterns allows for targeted monetisation strategies. High-spending players, or "whales," can be offered exclusive deals, while casual players might respond better to affordable IAPs.

Ethical Monetisation: Ethical monetisation practices prioritize transparency, fairness, and player well-being. Avoiding exploitative tactics like predatory pricing and ensuring players understand what they are purchasing can build trust and long-term loyalty.

In summary, mastering these key concepts is crucial for designing and implementing successful monetisation strategies in mobile games. Each concept plays a role in maximizing revenue, enhancing player experience, and ensuring the sustainability of the game.

1.5 Purpose and Structure of the Book

The purpose of this book is to provide a comprehensive guide to monetising mobile games, covering theoretical foundations, practical strategies, and case studies. It aims to equip game developers, marketers, and analysts with the knowledge and tools necessary to maximize revenue and enhance player experience.

The book is structured to take readers through a logical progression, starting with foundational concepts and moving towards advanced strategies and emerging trends. Each chapter builds on the previous ones, creating a cohesive and comprehensive resource.

Chapter 1 introduces the mobile game industry, its growth, and the importance of monetisation strategies. It sets the stage for the subsequent chapters by outlining key concepts and the purpose of the book.

Chapter 2 delves into the theoretical foundations of monetisation, exploring economic theories, psychological principles, and ethical considerations. Understanding these theories is essential for designing effective and ethical monetisation strategies.

Chapter 3 examines various monetisation models and strategies, including free-to-play, premium, freemium, and subscription models. It provides a comparative analysis to help developers choose the most suitable model for their games.

Chapter 4 focuses on in-game purchases and virtual goods, discussing types, pricing strategies, and balancing the in-game economy. It includes case studies of successful in-game purchase strategies.

Chapter 5 covers advertising in mobile games, exploring different types of ads, integration strategies, and revenue models. It also addresses challenges and opportunities in mobile game advertising.

Chapter 6 emphasizes the importance of player retention and engagement for monetisation. It discusses strategies for increasing retention, gamification techniques, and community building.

Chapter 7 looks at designing monetisation-friendly game mechanics, balancing fun and profit, and integrating monetisation into the game narrative. It highlights the importance of testing and iterating monetisation mechanics.

Chapter 8 explores user experience (UX) design principles for monetisation, ensuring a seamless purchase experience, and avoiding common UX pitfalls. It emphasizes the role of player personas and feedback in UX design.

Chapter 9 discusses data analytics and its role in monetisation, covering key metrics, tools, and case studies. It provides insights into interpreting and acting on data to optimize monetisation strategies.

Chapter 10 addresses legal and regulatory considerations, including privacy, consumer protection, and regional regulations. It offers guidance on navigating legal challenges in monetisation.

Chapter 11 provides global perspectives on monetisation, discussing trends, cultural differences, and localisation strategies. It includes success stories from various regions and insights into adapting to global market changes.

Chapter 12 examines monetisation in emerging technologies, such as AR, VR, blockchain, and AI. It explores innovations and future trends in mobile game monetisation.

Chapter 13 focuses on marketing and monetisation, covering marketing strategies, social media, influencer marketing, and measuring marketing effectiveness. It emphasizes the synergy between marketing and monetisation.

Chapter 14 presents case studies of successful mobile games, analyzing top-grossing games, lessons learned, and future trends predicted by these case studies.

Chapter 15 highlights the importance of player feedback and community management in monetisation. It discusses collecting, analyzing, and incorporating feedback into game development.

Chapter 16 addresses monetisation challenges and strategies for indie developers, including funding, financial planning, and marketing. It includes success stories of indie game monetisation.

Chapter 17 explores the future of mobile game monetisation, predicting market trends, potential disruptors, and evolving player expectations. It discusses the long-term sustainability of current models.

Chapter 18 provides tools and resources for developers, including monetisation platforms, analytics tools, best practices, and community opportunities. It emphasizes the importance of continuous learning.

Chapter 19 guides readers through building a monetisation strategy, covering steps to develop a plan, identifying target audiences, and implementing and testing strategies. It offers practical advice for reviewing and adapting monetisation plans.

Chapter 1: Introduction to Mobile Game Monetisation

Chapter 20 concludes the book with a recap of key points, reflections on the evolution of monetisation, and final thoughts on ethical practices. It encourages game developers to innovate and prioritize player experience in their monetisation efforts.

By following this structure, the book aims to provide a thorough understanding of mobile game monetisation, from foundational theories to practical applications and future trends.

Chapter 2: Theoretical Foundations of Monetisation

2.1 Economic Theories Relevant to Monetisation

Economic theories provide a crucial framework for understanding and developing monetisation strategies in mobile games. These theories help explain player behavior, market dynamics, and the impact of different monetisation models.

Supply and Demand: The basic principle of supply and demand applies to virtual goods and in-game purchases. Developers must balance the availability of virtual goods with player demand to optimize pricing and maximize revenue. Scarcity can increase the perceived value of items, encouraging players to spend more.

Price Elasticity: Price elasticity measures how sensitive player spending is to changes in price. Understanding the elasticity of different in-game items helps developers set prices that maximize revenue. Highly elastic items may see significant changes in sales volume with small price adjustments.

Utility Theory: Utility theory explains how players derive satisfaction or utility from virtual goods and in-game purchases. Developers can use this theory to design items and features that provide high utility, making players more willing to spend money.

Behavioral Economics: Behavioral economics explores the psychological factors that influence economic decisions. Concepts like loss aversion, where players are more motivated to avoid losses than achieve gains, can inform the design of monetisation strategies. For example, time-limited offers leverage loss aversion by creating a sense of urgency.

Game Theory: Game theory analyzes strategic interactions between players and developers. Understanding these interactions can help design monetisation strategies that encourage cooperative behavior, such as guilds or clans, where players spend to benefit their group.

Market Segmentation: Segmenting the market based on player behavior and preferences allows for targeted monetisation strategies. High-spending players, or "whales," can be offered exclusive items, while casual players might be enticed with affordable bundles or ads for rewards.

Network Effects: Network effects occur when the value of a game increases as more players join. Social features and multiplayer modes can enhance network effects, encouraging players to spend money to stay competitive or enhance their social interactions.

Auction Theory: Auction theory can be applied to in-game economies where players bid for rare items. This approach can drive up prices and increase revenue, but it requires careful design to ensure fairness and player satisfaction.

Dynamic Pricing: Dynamic pricing adjusts the cost of virtual goods based on player behavior and market conditions. This strategy can optimize revenue by charging higher prices during peak demand periods and offering discounts during slow periods.

Microtransactions: Microtransactions involve small, frequent purchases that can accumulate to significant revenue. Understanding the psychology behind microtransactions, such as the appeal of low-cost, incremental spending, is essential for effective monetisation.

Freemium Model: The freemium model combines free access to the game with optional paid content. This model relies on a large user base, with a small percentage of players making purchases. Understanding the balance between free and paid content is crucial for this model's success.

Subscription Model: Subscription models offer recurring revenue through regular payments for access to exclusive content or features. This model requires delivering consistent value to retain subscribers and prevent churn.

In summary, economic theories provide valuable insights into player behavior and market dynamics. Applying these theories to monetisation strategies can help developers optimize pricing, design appealing virtual goods, and create sustainable revenue models.

2.2 Psychological Principles in Monetisation

Psychological principles play a significant role in shaping monetisation strategies for mobile games. Understanding how players think, feel, and behave can help developers create engaging and profitable games.

Motivation: Players are motivated by various factors, including achievement, social interaction, and immersion. Designing monetisation strategies that tap into these motivations can enhance player engagement and spending. For example, offering exclusive items or rewards for achieving milestones can appeal to achievement-driven players.

Reward Systems: Reward systems leverage the psychology of reinforcement to encourage desired behaviors. Variable ratio schedules, where rewards are given after an unpredictable number of actions, can create a compelling loop that keeps players engaged and spending. Daily rewards and streak bonuses also encourage regular play and investment.

Instant Gratification: Instant gratification is the desire for immediate rewards. In-game purchases that provide instant benefits, such as power-ups or cosmetic items, appeal to this desire and can drive impulsive spending. Time-limited offers and flash sales can also leverage the need for instant gratification.

Loss Aversion: Loss aversion refers to the tendency to prefer avoiding losses over acquiring gains. Time-limited offers and exclusive items that might be removed from the store create a sense of potential loss, motivating players to make purchases to avoid missing out.

Social Proof: Social proof is the influence of others' actions on our behavior. Displaying purchase trends, popular items, or showing friends' in-game achievements can encourage players to spend money to fit in or compete. Leaderboards and social sharing features enhance this effect.

Endowment Effect: The endowment effect is the tendency to overvalue what we own. Allowing players to customize and personalize their virtual goods increases their perceived value, making them more willing to spend money to acquire or upgrade these items.

Commitment and Consistency: Players are more likely to continue a behavior if they have already committed to it. Offering small initial purchases or entry-level subscriptions can create a commitment that leads to higher spending over time. Progression systems that require consistent investment also leverage this principle.

Scarcity: Scarcity increases the perceived value of an item. Limited-time offers, exclusive items, and seasonal events create a sense of urgency and exclusivity, driving players to make purchases before they miss out.

Anchoring: Anchoring is the tendency to rely heavily on the first piece of information encountered. Displaying higher-priced items alongside regular items can make the latter appear more affordable and attractive. Bundles and discounts can also use anchoring to highlight savings.

Reciprocity: Reciprocity is the social norm of responding to a positive action with another positive action. Offering free gifts or trial access to premium features can create a sense of obligation in players, encouraging them to make purchases in return.

Gamification: Gamification incorporates game elements into non-game contexts to increase engagement and motivation. Applying gamification principles to monetisation, such as offering badges, achievements, and progress bars for spending, can make the process more enjoyable and rewarding.

Personalization: Personalization tailors the gaming experience to individual player preferences and behaviors. Personalized offers, recommendations, and rewards based on player data can increase the relevance and attractiveness of in-game purchases.

Habit Formation: Habit formation involves creating routines that become automatic over time. Daily quests, login rewards, and consistent content updates encourage regular play and spending, turning gaming into a habitual activity.

In conclusion, psychological principles provide powerful tools for designing effective monetisation strategies. By understanding and leveraging these principles, developers can create experiences that not only drive revenue but also enhance player satisfaction and engagement.

2.3 Behavioural Economics and Player Spending

Behavioural economics combines insights from psychology and economics to understand how people make decisions, often in ways that deviate from traditional economic theories. Applying behavioural economics to mobile game monetisation can reveal strategies to influence player spending.

Nudging: Nudging involves subtly guiding players towards desired actions without restricting their choices. For example, highlighting limited-time offers or displaying recommended purchases can nudge players towards spending money. Gentle reminders about expiring discounts or low stock can also be effective.

Framing Effects: Framing effects occur when the way information is presented influences decision-making. Presenting in-game purchases as opportunities to enhance the gaming experience, rather than just spending money, can make them more appealing. Positive framing, such as highlighting benefits rather than costs, can increase purchase rates.

Mental Accounting: Mental accounting refers to the way people categorize and treat money differently based on its source or intended use. Offering virtual currency in different packages or creating special "event" currencies can encourage players to spend more. Players may be more willing to spend virtual currency they earned in-game rather than real money.

Sunk Cost Fallacy: The sunk cost fallacy is the tendency to continue investing in something because of the resources already spent. Players who have already spent money or time in a game are more likely to keep spending to justify their previous investments. Developers can leverage this by offering progression-based purchases or rewards.

Hyperbolic Discounting: Hyperbolic discounting is the tendency to prefer smaller, immediate rewards over larger, delayed ones. In-game purchases that offer instant benefits, such as boosts or unlocks, can be more attractive than long-term advantages. Time-limited offers also capitalize on this preference for immediacy.

Default Options: Setting default options can influence player behavior. For example, pre-selecting higher-tier purchase options or automatically enrolling players in subscription trials can increase the likelihood of these choices. Players are more likely to go with default settings if they require less effort.

Overchoice: Too many options can overwhelm players and lead to decision paralysis. Simplifying the purchase process by offering curated bundles, popular items, or personalized recommendations can make decision-making easier and increase sales.

Social Norms: Social norms influence behavior through the perceived expectations of others. Highlighting popular purchases or showing what friends are buying can create a sense of social pressure to conform, encouraging spending. Social features like leaderboards and achievements can also leverage social norms.

Temporal Landmarks: Temporal landmarks, such as holidays, events, or new game updates, can create natural opportunities for spending. Special events, seasonal offers, and anniversary sales capitalize on these moments, making players more likely to spend.

Emotional Triggers: Emotions play a significant role in decision-making. Creating emotional experiences, such as through compelling narratives, characters, or events, can increase player attachment and willingness to spend. Offering purchases that enhance these emotional connections, like story expansions or character skins, can be effective.

Anchoring and Adjustment: Players often rely on initial information (anchors) when making decisions. Displaying higher-priced items alongside regular items can make the latter seem more affordable. Discounts and sales also use anchoring by showing original prices to highlight savings.

Endowment Effect: The endowment effect makes players value items they own more highly. Allowing players to earn or customize items before offering upgrades or enhancements can increase their perceived value, making them more likely to spend.

Feedback Loops: Positive feedback loops, where player actions lead to rewards, which in turn encourage more actions, can drive spending. Rewarding purchases with bonuses, exclusive items, or progression boosts creates a cycle of continuous engagement and investment.

In summary, behavioural economics provides valuable insights into player spending behavior. By applying these principles, developers can design monetisation strategies that resonate with players' psychological tendencies, leading to increased engagement and revenue.

2.4 Game Theory in Monetisation Strategies

Game theory is the study of strategic interactions and decision-making between players and entities. It offers valuable insights into designing monetisation strategies that optimize player engagement and revenue generation.

Prisoner's Dilemma: In the context of multiplayer games, the prisoner's dilemma illustrates the tension between cooperation and competition. Developers can design monetisation strategies that encourage players to collaborate for mutual benefit. For example, guilds or clans can have shared goals that require collective spending, such as unlocking group rewards or bonuses.

Zero-Sum and Non-Zero-Sum Games: In zero-sum games, one player's gain is another's loss. However, most mobile games are non-zero-sum, where multiple players can benefit simultaneously. Designing monetisation strategies that create win-win scenarios, such as trading or gifting virtual goods, can enhance player satisfaction and spending.

Tit-for-Tat: The tit-for-tat strategy involves reciprocating actions. In monetisation, this can be implemented through reward systems where players are encouraged to spend by receiving gifts or bonuses in return. For example, rewarding players for their first purchase or offering referral bonuses can create a positive feedback loop.

Nash Equilibrium: Nash equilibrium occurs when players reach a stable strategy where no one benefits from changing their choice unilaterally. In monetisation, developers can create balanced ecosystems where spending benefits all players equally. Ensuring fair competition and balanced gameplay encourages consistent spending across the player base.

Auction Theory: Auction theory can be applied to in-game economies where players bid for rare items or privileges. Implementing auction systems can drive up the perceived value of virtual goods, leading to higher spending. Developers must ensure fairness and transparency to maintain player trust.

Public Goods Game: The public goods game involves contributions to a shared resource. In games, this can be applied to community-driven goals, such as unlocking new content or events through collective spending. Players contribute individually but benefit collectively, fostering a sense of community and shared achievement.

Repeated Games: Repeated games involve ongoing interactions with the same players, where past actions influence future decisions. Implementing loyalty programs or subscription models leverages this concept by rewarding consistent spending and engagement over time.

Mechanism Design: Mechanism design involves creating systems or incentives to achieve desired outcomes. Developers can design monetisation mechanisms that align player behavior with revenue goals. For example, tiered rewards or progressive discounts can incentivize higher spending.

Pareto Efficiency: Pareto efficiency occurs when no player can be made better off without making another player worse off. Designing monetisation strategies that maximize overall player welfare without disadvantaging others can create a balanced and fair game environment. Ensuring that purchases do not create significant power imbalances is crucial.

Evolutionary Game Theory: Evolutionary game theory studies how strategies evolve over time. Developers can use this concept to adapt monetisation strategies based on player behavior and feedback. Continuous updates and iterations based on data insights ensure that monetisation remains effective and relevant.

Social Preferences: Players often consider fairness, reciprocity, and altruism in their decisions. Designing monetisation strategies that reflect these social preferences can enhance player satisfaction and spending. Offering charity events, where a portion of proceeds goes to real-world causes, can resonate with socially conscious players.

Signaling: Signaling involves actions that convey information. In monetisation, developers can use signaling to highlight the value of purchases. For example, exclusive items or premium memberships can signal status and prestige, encouraging players to spend to attain these symbols.

In conclusion, game theory provides a robust framework for understanding strategic interactions and decision-making in mobile games. By applying game theory principles, developers can design monetisation strategies that optimize player engagement, satisfaction, and revenue.

2.5 Ethics in Game Monetisation

Ethical considerations are increasingly important in game monetisation, as players and regulators demand transparency, fairness, and responsibility from developers. Ethical monetisation practices not only build trust and loyalty but also ensure long-term sustainability and compliance with legal standards.

Transparency: Transparency involves clearly communicating the terms and conditions of in-game purchases, virtual goods, and subscriptions. Players should understand what they are buying, how much it costs, and any potential impacts on gameplay. Providing clear and concise information helps build trust and reduces the risk of disputes.

Fair Pricing: Fair pricing ensures that in-game purchases offer value for money and do not exploit players. Developers should avoid setting excessively high prices for essential items or creating pay-to-win scenarios where spending money provides unfair advantages. Offering a range of affordable options caters to different budgets and player preferences.

Informed Consent: Informed consent requires players to make purchase decisions with full knowledge and understanding. Implementing measures like confirmation screens, spending limits, and parental controls helps prevent unintentional or unauthorized purchases, particularly for younger players.

Avoiding Exploitative Practices: Exploitative practices, such as predatory pricing, loot boxes with gambling-like mechanics, and aggressive push notifications, can harm players and damage a game's reputation. Developers should prioritize player well-being and avoid tactics that exploit psychological vulnerabilities.

Data Privacy: Protecting player data and privacy is crucial in ethical monetisation. Developers must comply with data protection regulations, such as GDPR and CCPA, and ensure that player data is collected, stored, and used responsibly. Players should have control over their data and be informed about how it is used.

Balancing Monetisation and Gameplay: Ethical monetisation balances revenue generation with a positive player experience. In-game purchases and ads should not disrupt gameplay or create frustration. Developers should strive to enhance the gaming experience through monetisation, rather than detract from it.

Parental Controls and Age Appropriateness: Implementing parental controls and ensuring age-appropriate content helps protect younger players. Games targeting children should have safeguards to prevent excessive spending and provide parents with tools to manage their child's gaming activities.

Community and Social Responsibility: Ethical monetisation practices consider the broader impact on the player community and society. Developers can engage in social responsibility initiatives, such as charity events or educational content, to contribute positively to the community. Building a supportive and inclusive player community also enhances long-term engagement.

Regulatory Compliance: Compliance with legal and regulatory standards is a fundamental aspect of ethical monetisation. Developers must stay informed about relevant laws and regulations in different regions and ensure that their monetisation practices adhere to these standards. This includes addressing issues related to gambling, consumer protection, and advertising.

Player Feedback and Adaptation: Listening to player feedback and adapting monetisation strategies accordingly is essential for ethical practices. Regularly collecting and analyzing feedback helps identify pain points and areas for improvement. Engaging with the player community and being responsive to their concerns fosters trust and loyalty.

Sustainability: Long-term sustainability is a key consideration in ethical monetisation. Developers should focus on creating games that provide ongoing value and enjoyment, rather than prioritizing short-term profits. Sustainable monetisation practices ensure that players remain engaged and satisfied over the long term.

Educational Resources: Providing educational resources about responsible spending and gaming habits can empower players to make informed decisions. Developers can include tips and guidelines within the game or on their websites to promote healthy gaming behaviors.

In summary, ethical considerations in game monetisation are essential for building trust, maintaining player satisfaction, and ensuring long-term success. By prioritizing transparency, fairness, and responsibility, developers can create monetisation strategies that benefit both players and the business.

Chapter 3: Monetisation Models and Strategies

3.1 Free-to-Play (F2P) Model

The Free-to-Play (F2P) model has revolutionized the mobile gaming industry by offering games for free while monetizing through in-game purchases and advertisements. This model removes the initial barrier to entry, allowing a wider audience to access the game, which in turn increases the potential for revenue generation through other means.

One of the primary advantages of the F2P model is its ability to attract a large user base quickly. By eliminating the upfront cost, more players are willing to download and try the game. This larger player base can lead to increased social sharing, word-of-mouth promotion, and higher rankings in app stores, further boosting visibility and downloads.

In-game purchases, or microtransactions, are a cornerstone of the F2P model. These purchases can range from cosmetic items, such as skins and outfits, to functional items that enhance gameplay, such as power-ups, extra lives, or faster progression. Players can choose to spend money to enhance their gaming experience, providing a steady stream of revenue for developers.

Another key component of the F2P model is advertising. Many F2P games integrate ads in various forms, including banner ads, interstitial ads, and rewarded videos. Rewarded videos, in particular, have gained popularity as they offer players in-game rewards, such as extra lives or currency, in exchange for watching an advertisement. This creates a win-win situation where players receive benefits and developers earn ad revenue.

However, the F2P model is not without its challenges. One significant challenge is balancing monetization with player satisfaction. Over-monetization can lead to player frustration and churn, while under-monetization can result in insufficient revenue to sustain the game. Developers must find the right balance to ensure a positive player experience while maximizing revenue.

Retention is another critical factor in the success of F2P games. High retention rates mean more opportunities for players to make in-game purchases and view ads. Strategies to improve retention include regular content updates, engaging gameplay mechanics, and effective onboarding processes that help new players quickly understand and enjoy the game.

The use of analytics is crucial in optimizing the F2P model. By analyzing player behavior, developers can identify patterns and trends that inform decisions about game design, monetization strategies, and marketing campaigns. Key metrics to monitor include daily active users (DAU), average revenue per user (ARPU), and lifetime value (LTV) of players.

In addition to in-game purchases and ads, some F2P games offer subscription models. Subscriptions can provide a steady and predictable revenue stream and often include exclusive benefits such as ad-free gameplay, special items, or early access to new content. Offering a combination of free content and optional subscriptions can cater to both casual players and dedicated fans.

The success of the F2P model also depends on effective user acquisition strategies. These strategies can include app store optimization (ASO), social media marketing, influencer partnerships, and paid advertising campaigns. By attracting a large and engaged user base, developers can increase their chances of generating significant revenue.

Despite the competition in the F2P market, there are numerous success stories. Games like "Fortnite," "Clash of Clans," and "Candy Crush Saga" have achieved massive success with the F2P model, generating billions in revenue through in-game purchases and ads. These games offer valuable lessons in balancing monetization with player satisfaction and using data-driven strategies to optimize performance.

In conclusion, the Free-to-Play model offers a powerful framework for monetizing mobile games. By attracting a large user base and leveraging in-game purchases, ads, and subscriptions, developers can generate substantial revenue. However, success requires a careful balance between monetization and player satisfaction, effective retention strategies, and data-driven decision-making.

3.2 Premium and Freemium Models

The premium model, also known as pay-to-play, requires players to purchase the game upfront before gaining access to its content. This traditional approach offers several advantages and challenges compared to other monetization strategies.

One of the main benefits of the premium model is the immediate revenue it generates. Since players must pay to download the game, developers receive upfront payments, providing a predictable income stream. This can be particularly beneficial for indie developers and smaller studios that rely on initial sales to fund development and marketing efforts.

Premium games often focus on delivering a high-quality, complete experience. Without the pressure to include in-game purchases or ads, developers can concentrate on creating engaging and polished gameplay. This can result in higher player satisfaction and better reviews, which, in turn, can boost sales and visibility in app stores.

However, the premium model also presents challenges, primarily in user acquisition. The upfront cost can be a significant barrier for potential players, especially in a market saturated with free alternatives. To overcome this, developers need to invest in effective marketing campaigns and build strong brand recognition to convince players that their game is worth the price.

The freemium model combines elements of both free-to-play and premium models. It offers a base game for free while charging for additional content or features. This hybrid approach aims to attract a wide audience with the free version while monetizing through optional purchases.

In the freemium model, the free version typically includes basic gameplay, while premium features or content are locked behind a paywall. This can include additional levels, characters, customization options, or advanced gameplay mechanics. By offering a taste of the game for free, developers can hook players and incentivize them to spend money on premium content.

One of the key advantages of the freemium model is its ability to attract a large user base quickly. The free version lowers the barrier to entry, allowing more players to try the game. This can lead to increased word-of-mouth promotion, higher app store rankings, and a larger potential market for premium purchases.

Monetizing a freemium game requires a careful balance between free and paid content. Developers must ensure that the free version is enjoyable and engaging enough to retain players, while also providing compelling reasons to upgrade to the premium version. This can involve strategic use of in-game prompts, limited-time offers, and exclusive content to encourage spending.

Another important aspect of the freemium model is the use of analytics to understand player behavior and optimize monetization strategies. By tracking metrics such as conversion rates, user engagement, and purchase patterns, developers can identify opportunities to improve the game and increase revenue. Data-driven insights can guide decisions on content updates, pricing strategies, and marketing campaigns.

A successful example of the freemium model is the game "Angry Birds." The initial version of the game was free to download, but players could purchase additional levels and power-ups. This approach allowed the game to reach a broad audience while generating significant revenue through in-app purchases. The success of "Angry Birds" demonstrates the potential of the freemium model to combine wide accessibility with effective monetization.

In conclusion, both the premium and freemium models offer unique advantages and challenges. The premium model provides immediate revenue and allows for a focus on quality, but may face barriers in user acquisition. The freemium model attracts a large audience with free content and monetizes through optional purchases, but requires a careful balance to ensure player satisfaction and revenue generation. By understanding the strengths and weaknesses of each approach, developers can choose the right model for their game and market.

3.3 Subscription Models

Subscription models have gained traction in the mobile gaming industry as a viable monetization strategy. Unlike traditional models where players pay once or make in-game purchases, subscriptions offer recurring revenue by charging players a regular fee, typically monthly or annually, for access to premium content or features.

One of the primary advantages of subscription models is the steady and predictable revenue stream they provide. This recurring income can be particularly beneficial for developers, allowing for more accurate financial planning and sustained investment in game development and updates. The stability of subscription revenue can also support long-term projects and continuous improvement of the game.

Subscriptions can enhance player retention by providing ongoing value. When players subscribe, they are more likely to stay engaged with the game to make the most of their investment. This can lead to higher retention rates and a more dedicated player base. Offering exclusive content, such as new levels, characters, or special events, can further incentivize players to maintain their subscriptions.

Another benefit of subscription models is the ability to offer a premium, ad-free experience. Many players are willing to pay a recurring fee to enjoy a game without interruptions from ads. This can improve the overall player experience and satisfaction, potentially leading to positive reviews and word-of-mouth promotion.

Implementing a subscription model requires careful consideration of pricing and value proposition. Developers need to strike a balance between offering enough value to justify the subscription cost while keeping the price attractive to players. This can involve tiered subscription plans, where higher-priced tiers offer more benefits, allowing players to choose the level of investment that suits them.

Marketing subscriptions effectively is crucial for success. Clear communication of the benefits and exclusive content available to subscribers can help convince players to sign up. Offering free trials or limited-time discounts can also be effective strategies to encourage initial subscriptions and allow players to experience the value firsthand.

Subscriptions can also integrate with other monetization strategies. For example, a game might offer a free version with ads and in-app purchases, while the subscription plan provides an ad-free experience and additional premium content. This hybrid approach can cater to different player preferences and maximize revenue potential.

Analyzing subscription metrics is essential to optimize the model. Key metrics to monitor include subscription conversion rates, churn rates (the rate at which subscribers cancel), and lifetime value (LTV) of subscribers. By understanding these metrics, developers can identify areas for improvement and implement strategies to increase retention and reduce churn.

A notable success story of the subscription model is "Apple Arcade." Apple Arcade offers a wide range of premium games for a monthly fee, providing an ad-free and in-app purchase-free experience. This model has attracted a significant number of subscribers, demonstrating the appeal of a curated collection of high-quality games under a subscription plan.

In addition to individual game subscriptions, there is potential for cross-game subscription services. Platforms that offer access to multiple games for a single subscription fee can provide added value to players and create a more robust revenue stream for developers. This approach leverages the concept of a gaming ecosystem, where players can enjoy a variety of games within a single subscription.

In conclusion, subscription models offer a promising monetization strategy for mobile games. The recurring revenue stream, enhanced player retention, and potential for an ad-free experience are significant advantages. However, success requires careful pricing, effective marketing, and continuous analysis of subscription metrics. By delivering ongoing value and exclusive content, developers can build a loyal subscriber base and achieve long-term financial stability.

3.4 Hybrid Monetisation Models

Hybrid monetization models combine multiple revenue streams to maximize a game's earning potential while catering to diverse player preferences. By integrating elements of free-to-play, premium, freemium, and subscription models, developers can create a flexible and adaptable monetization strategy.

One common hybrid approach is to offer a free version of the game with optional in-app purchases and a premium, ad-free version for a one-time fee. This model caters to players who prefer a free experience supported by ads and those willing to pay for an enhanced, uninterrupted experience. This dual offering can increase the game's overall reach and revenue potential.

Another effective hybrid strategy is combining free-to-play mechanics with subscription options. In this model, the base game is free, but players can subscribe to gain access to exclusive content, faster progression, or premium features. This approach leverages the large user base attracted by the free game and provides an additional revenue stream through subscriptions.

Season passes and battle passes are popular hybrid models in many games. These passes offer a mix of free and paid content, typically tied to a specific timeframe or season. Players can earn rewards through gameplay, with additional premium rewards available to those who purchase the pass. This model encourages ongoing engagement and spending, as players are incentivized to complete challenges and earn exclusive items.

Hybrid monetization can also involve combining in-game advertisements with in-app purchases. For example, a game might offer rewarded video ads that provide players with in-game currency or items in exchange for watching an ad. This creates a balance where non-paying players can still progress and enjoy the game, while those who prefer not to watch ads can make purchases instead.

The use of analytics is crucial in optimizing hybrid monetization models. By tracking player behavior, developers can identify which monetization elements are most effective and make data-driven decisions to refine their strategy. Metrics such as ad engagement rates, in-app purchase conversion rates, and subscription renewal rates provide valuable insights into player preferences and spending habits.

Effective communication and transparency are key to the success of hybrid models. Players should understand the different monetization options available and the benefits of each. Clear messaging about what is included in free versus paid content helps manage player expectations and reduce potential frustration.

Hybrid monetization models also allow for greater experimentation and flexibility. Developers can test different combinations of revenue streams to see what works best for their game and audience. This iterative approach enables continuous improvement and adaptation to changing market trends and player preferences.

One example of a successful hybrid model is the game "Fortnite." Fortnite offers a free-to-play battle royale mode with in-app purchases for cosmetic items. Additionally, it features a battle pass that players can purchase to unlock exclusive rewards throughout a season. This combination of free gameplay, optional purchases, and seasonal content has contributed to the game's massive success and revenue generation.

The hybrid model can also be tailored to different regions and markets. By understanding cultural differences and local player behavior, developers can adjust their monetization strategy to suit specific audiences. This localization can involve varying the types of in-app purchases, subscription offerings, or ad formats used in different regions.

In conclusion, hybrid monetization models provide a versatile and adaptable approach to generating revenue in mobile games. By combining elements of various monetization strategies, developers can cater to a wide range of player preferences and maximize their earning potential. Success requires effective use of analytics, clear communication, and a willingness to experiment and adapt. Hybrid models offer the flexibility needed to thrive in the competitive and ever-evolving mobile gaming market.

3.5 Comparative Analysis of Monetisation Models

A comparative analysis of different monetization models highlights their unique advantages, challenges, and suitability for various types of games and audiences. Understanding these differences can help developers choose the best strategy for their specific needs and goals.

The Free-to-Play (F2P) model is highly effective for attracting a large user base quickly. By offering the game for free, developers can reach a wider audience, increasing the potential for in-game purchases and ad revenue. However, the challenge lies in balancing monetization with player satisfaction to avoid alienating users.

Premium models, requiring an upfront purchase, provide immediate revenue and allow developers to focus on delivering a high-quality experience without the need for ongoing monetization. This model works well for games with strong brand recognition or those offering a unique and complete experience. The primary challenge is convincing players to pay upfront, especially in a market dominated by free alternatives.

Freemium models offer a base game for free with optional premium content. This hybrid approach combines the accessibility of F2P with the revenue potential of premium features. It requires a careful balance between free and paid content to ensure player engagement while encouraging spending. Freemium models can attract a large user base and generate revenue through a mix of in-game purchases and ads.

Subscription models provide a steady and predictable revenue stream by charging players a recurring fee for access to premium content. This model can enhance player retention by offering ongoing value and exclusive benefits. However, success depends on delivering continuous updates and maintaining a compelling value proposition to justify the subscription cost.

Hybrid monetization models combine elements of various strategies to create a flexible and adaptable approach. By integrating F2P, premium, freemium, and subscription elements, developers can cater to diverse player preferences and maximize revenue potential. This model allows for greater experimentation and adaptation but requires careful analysis and optimization to balance the different revenue streams effectively.

When comparing these models, several factors should be considered:

1. **Audience**: Understanding the target audience is crucial. Casual gamers may prefer F2P or freemium models, while hardcore gamers might be more willing to pay upfront for a premium experience. Subscription models can appeal to players seeking ongoing engagement and exclusive content.
2. **Game Type**: The genre and design of the game influence the suitable monetization model. For instance, social and multiplayer games often thrive with F2P and freemium models, while narrative-driven games might be better suited for premium or subscription models.
3. **Market Trends**: Staying informed about market trends and player preferences can guide the choice of monetization strategy. Analyzing successful games in similar genres can provide insights into effective models and potential pitfalls.
4. **Revenue Goals**: Developers should consider their financial objectives. F2P models can generate high revenue through volume, while premium models offer immediate income. Subscription models provide long-term stability, and hybrid models offer a balance of multiple revenue streams.
5. **Retention and Engagement**: The ability to retain and engage players impacts the success of the monetization model. High retention rates are essential for F2P, freemium, and subscription models to maximize revenue through ongoing engagement and spending.
6. **Development Resources**: The resources available for development and marketing play a role in choosing the monetization model. Premium and subscription models may require significant upfront investment in quality and content, while F2P and freemium models need continuous updates and support.

In conclusion, each monetization model has its strengths and challenges. The choice of model depends on various factors, including the target audience, game type, market trends, revenue goals, retention and engagement strategies, and available resources. By understanding these factors and conducting a comparative analysis, developers can select the most suitable monetization strategy for their game, maximizing both player satisfaction and revenue potential.

Chapter 4: In-Game Purchases and Virtual Goods

4.1 Types of In-Game Purchases

In-game purchases, also known as microtransactions, are a fundamental aspect of modern mobile game monetization. These purchases allow players to buy virtual goods and services within the game, enhancing their experience and providing developers with a steady revenue stream. There are several types of in-game purchases, each serving different purposes and appealing to various player motivations.

1. **Consumable Items**: These are items that players can use once or for a limited time. Examples include health potions, power-ups, and in-game currency. Consumable items are often priced affordably, encouraging frequent purchases. They cater to players who seek immediate benefits or need a quick boost to overcome challenging levels.
2. **Non-Consumable Items**: Unlike consumable items, non-consumable items are permanent and can be used indefinitely. Examples include character skins, outfits, and decorative items for avatars or game environments. These items often appeal to players who enjoy customization and personalization, allowing them to express their unique style within the game.
3. **Durable Goods**: These items provide long-term benefits and can enhance gameplay over an extended period. Examples include upgraded weapons, enhanced abilities, and permanent buffs. Durable goods are typically more expensive than consumable items and are often positioned as premium purchases.
4. **Unlockables**: Some games offer content that can be unlocked through in-game purchases. This can include new levels, characters, storylines, or game modes. Unlockables provide players with additional content and extend the game's longevity, offering a compelling reason to spend money.
5. **Cosmetic Items**: These items change the appearance of characters, vehicles, or environments without affecting gameplay. Examples include skins, outfits, emotes, and decorative items. Cosmetic items are popular because they allow players to personalize their gaming experience and stand out in social or multiplayer settings.
6. **Loot Boxes**: These are virtual containers that players can purchase, which contain random items. Loot boxes often include a mix of consumable, non-consumable, and cosmetic items. The randomness adds an element of excitement and anticipation, similar to opening a pack of trading cards. However, the use of loot boxes has faced criticism and regulatory scrutiny due to concerns about gambling-like mechanics.
7. **Subscriptions and Battle Passes**: Some games offer subscription services or battle passes that provide ongoing benefits over a set period. Subscribers might receive regular deliveries of in-game currency, exclusive items, or access to premium content. Battle passes often include tiers of rewards that players can unlock by completing challenges and progressing through the game.

8. **Gacha Mechanics**: Common in many mobile games, especially those from East Asia, gacha mechanics involve players spending in-game currency to receive random characters, items, or equipment. The appeal lies in the chance to obtain rare and powerful items, encouraging repeated spending.
9. **Time-Limited Offers**: These are special deals available for a limited time, often featuring discounted items, exclusive bundles, or rare goods. Time-limited offers create a sense of urgency, prompting players to make quick purchasing decisions to avoid missing out.
10. **Boosters and Accelerators**: These items speed up progress or provide temporary advantages. Examples include experience boosters, resource multipliers, and time reducers for building or crafting. Boosters and accelerators appeal to players looking to advance quickly without investing additional time.

Developers need to consider several factors when implementing in-game purchases. Pricing strategy, item balance, and the perceived value of virtual goods are crucial in determining the success of these purchases. Overpricing or under-delivering can lead to player dissatisfaction and reduced spending.

Ethical considerations are also important. Developers should ensure that in-game purchases do not create a "pay-to-win" environment, where players who spend money have a significant advantage over those who do not. Maintaining a fair and enjoyable experience for all players is essential for long-term success.

In conclusion, in-game purchases encompass a wide range of items and services, each catering to different player motivations and preferences. By understanding the types of in-game purchases and implementing them thoughtfully, developers can create a compelling monetization strategy that enhances the player experience and drives revenue.

4.2 Virtual Goods: Definition and Importance

Virtual goods are digital items that players can purchase, earn, or trade within a game. These goods can include a wide range of items, from cosmetic enhancements to functional assets that impact gameplay. Understanding the definition and importance of virtual goods is crucial for developers looking to monetize their games effectively.

Virtual goods are often categorized into two main types: cosmetic and functional. Cosmetic goods alter the appearance of characters, items, or environments without affecting gameplay mechanics. Examples include skins, outfits, emotes, and decorative items. These goods appeal to players' desires for personalization and self-expression, allowing them to customize their in-game experience.

Functional virtual goods, on the other hand, provide tangible benefits that can enhance gameplay. These goods can include power-ups, weapons, armor, abilities, and other items that directly impact a player's performance or progress in the game. Functional goods are often sought after by players looking to gain an advantage or improve their chances of success.

The importance of virtual goods in mobile game monetization cannot be overstated. They serve as a primary revenue stream for many free-to-play and freemium games, allowing developers to generate income without charging for the initial download. By offering a variety of virtual goods, developers can cater to different player preferences and encourage spending.

Virtual goods also play a significant role in player engagement and retention. The availability of desirable items can motivate players to spend more time in the game, striving to earn or purchase their favorite goods. This increased engagement can lead to higher retention rates, as players are continually drawn back to the game to acquire new items and enhance their experience.

In addition to direct sales, virtual goods can drive revenue through other monetization strategies, such as advertising and subscriptions. For example, rewarded video ads can offer players virtual goods as incentives for watching ads, creating a win-win situation where players receive valuable items, and developers earn ad revenue.

The social aspect of virtual goods is another important factor. In multiplayer and social games, players often use virtual goods to showcase their achievements, status, and style to others. This social interaction can create a sense of community and competition, further enhancing player engagement and encouraging spending on desirable items.

Implementing virtual goods requires careful consideration of several factors:

1. **Balancing**: It's essential to ensure that virtual goods do not disrupt the game's balance or create a pay-to-win environment. Players should feel that their purchases are valuable but not mandatory for enjoying the game.
2. **Pricing Strategy**: Setting the right price for virtual goods is crucial. Prices should reflect the perceived value of the items and be accessible to a broad range of players. Offering items at various price points can cater to different spending levels.
3. **Scarcity and Exclusivity**: Limited-time offers, rare items, and exclusive goods can create a sense of urgency and increase their desirability. Players are often willing to spend more on items that are perceived as rare or unique.
4. **Customization and Personalization**: Offering a wide variety of cosmetic goods allows players to express their individuality and customize their experience. Regularly updating the available items can keep the game fresh and exciting.
5. **Ethical Considerations**: Developers should be mindful of ethical considerations, ensuring that virtual goods do not exploit players or create unhealthy spending habits. Transparency about the nature of virtual goods and their impact on gameplay is important for maintaining player trust.

In conclusion, virtual goods are a vital component of mobile game monetization, offering both cosmetic and functional benefits to players. By understanding the importance of virtual goods and implementing them thoughtfully, developers can enhance player engagement, retention, and revenue, creating a sustainable and enjoyable gaming experience.

4.3 Pricing Strategies for Virtual Goods

Pricing strategies for virtual goods are critical to the success of in-game purchases and overall monetization. Setting the right price involves understanding player psychology, market trends, and the perceived value of items. Here are several effective pricing strategies that developers can use to optimize revenue from virtual goods.

1. **Tiered Pricing**: Offering virtual goods at various price points can cater to different segments of players. Lower-priced items can attract casual spenders, while higher-priced, premium items can appeal to more dedicated players. This approach allows developers to maximize revenue from a diverse player base.
2. **Anchoring**: Anchoring involves setting a high-priced item as a reference point to make other items seem more affordable by comparison. For example, if a premium skin is priced at $50, a $10 skin may seem like a bargain. This strategy can influence player perception and encourage purchases of mid-range items.
3. **Dynamic Pricing**: Dynamic pricing adjusts the cost of virtual goods based on various factors, such as player behavior, in-game events, or time of purchase. For instance, prices might be lowered during special promotions or increased for limited-edition items. Dynamic pricing can create a sense of urgency and capitalize on players' willingness to spend at specific moments.
4. **Freemium and Premium Tiers**: In a freemium model, the base game is free, and players can purchase virtual goods to enhance their experience. Premium tiers can offer exclusive items, faster progression, or additional content. This strategy provides a clear value proposition for spending and can increase overall revenue.
5. **Bundling**: Bundling involves offering multiple items together at a discounted price. For example, a bundle might include a weapon, armor, and a character skin at a lower cost than purchasing each item individually. Bundles can encourage players to spend more by providing perceived value and convenience.
6. **Psychological Pricing**: Psychological pricing leverages human perception to make prices more appealing. Common techniques include pricing items just below whole numbers (e.g., $9.99 instead of $10) and using smaller currency units (e.g., 99 cents). These strategies can make prices appear more attractive and encourage impulse purchases.
7. **Scarcity and Time-Limited Offers**: Creating a sense of scarcity or urgency can drive sales. Limited-time offers, flash sales, and exclusive items that are only available for a short period can prompt players to make quick purchasing decisions to avoid missing out.
8. **Customizable Pricing**: Allowing players to set their own price within a range can be an innovative approach. This strategy can be particularly effective for charitable events or community-driven content, where players feel more involved in the purchasing process.
9. **Regional Pricing**: Adjusting prices based on regional economic conditions can make virtual goods more accessible to players in different parts of the world. This strategy ensures that items are affordable and competitive in various markets, increasing the potential for global revenue.
10. **Subscription Discounts**: Offering discounts on virtual goods for subscribers can add value to subscription plans and incentivize players to commit to recurring payments. This approach can enhance both subscription and in-game purchase revenue streams.

11. **Event-Based Pricing**: Special events, holidays, and in-game milestones provide opportunities for unique pricing strategies. Offering exclusive items or discounts during these events can boost sales and create excitement among players.
12. **Testing and Optimization**: Continuous testing and optimization of pricing strategies are essential. A/B testing different price points, analyzing sales data, and gathering player feedback can help developers refine their pricing approach to maximize revenue and player satisfaction.

In conclusion, effective pricing strategies for virtual goods require a deep understanding of player psychology, market trends, and the perceived value of items. By implementing tiered pricing, anchoring, dynamic pricing, bundling, and other strategies, developers can optimize their revenue while ensuring a positive player experience. Continuous testing and adaptation are key to finding the right balance and maintaining a successful monetization strategy.

4.4 Balancing In-Game Economy

Balancing the in-game economy is crucial for creating a fair and engaging experience that keeps players invested and willing to spend. A well-balanced economy ensures that virtual goods, currencies, and rewards are appropriately valued and that the game remains enjoyable for both paying and non-paying players. Here are several strategies for achieving this balance.

1. **Fair Pricing of Virtual Goods**: It's important to price virtual goods in a way that reflects their value and effort required to obtain them. Overpricing can lead to frustration and reduced sales, while underpricing can devalue items and impact revenue. Regularly reviewing and adjusting prices based on player feedback and sales data can help maintain balance.
2. **Multiple Currencies**: Many games use multiple types of in-game currency, such as premium currency (purchased with real money) and standard currency (earned through gameplay). Balancing the acquisition rates and uses of these currencies ensures that players feel rewarded for their time while providing monetization opportunities for developers.
3. **Reward Systems**: Implementing a robust reward system that offers meaningful and achievable goals is essential. Daily rewards, achievements, and event-based bonuses can keep players engaged and motivated to continue playing. Ensuring that rewards are valuable and attainable without feeling too grindy is key to maintaining player satisfaction.
4. **In-Game Economy Models**: Utilizing various in-game economy models, such as supply and demand, can create a dynamic and engaging experience. For example, the availability of certain items might change based on player actions, creating a sense of impact and immersion. Balancing these models requires careful planning and ongoing adjustments.
5. **Balancing Progression**: Ensuring that the game's progression system is balanced is critical. Players should feel a sense of accomplishment as they progress, without hitting paywalls or encountering significant difficulty spikes that push them towards spending money. Gradual and rewarding progression keeps players engaged and reduces frustration.

6. **Avoiding Pay-to-Win**: It's important to avoid creating a pay-to-win environment where spending money gives players a significant advantage over others. Balancing competitive elements and ensuring that skill and strategy are the primary determinants of success can help maintain a fair and enjoyable experience for all players.
7. **Marketplaces and Trading**: If the game includes player-to-player trading or marketplaces, ensuring a balanced and fair economy is crucial. Developers should monitor the market for inflation, item duplication, and unfair trading practices. Implementing measures to prevent exploitation and maintain a stable economy is essential.
8. **Regular Updates and Adjustments**: The in-game economy should be dynamic and adaptable. Regular updates that introduce new content, adjust item values, and respond to player feedback can help keep the economy balanced and the game fresh. Transparency with players about changes and the reasons behind them fosters trust and engagement.
9. **Data-Driven Decisions**: Leveraging data analytics to monitor the in-game economy is crucial for making informed decisions. Analyzing player behavior, spending patterns, and item usage can provide insights into potential imbalances and areas for improvement. Data-driven adjustments ensure that changes are effective and based on actual player activity.
10. **Community Feedback**: Engaging with the player community and gathering feedback is invaluable for balancing the in-game economy. Players often have insights into what feels fair and enjoyable. Incorporating their feedback into the decision-making process helps create a more balanced and player-centric experience.
11. **Economic Sinks**: Implementing economic sinks, or mechanisms that remove currency from the game, can help prevent inflation and maintain balance. Examples include repair costs, upgrade fees, and limited-time events that encourage spending. Properly designed economic sinks ensure that the in-game economy remains healthy and sustainable.
12. **Testing and Iteration**: Continuous testing and iteration are key to maintaining a balanced in-game economy. Developers should conduct regular playtests, gather player feedback, and analyze economic data to identify and address any imbalances. Iterative improvements help create a stable and enjoyable experience.

In conclusion, balancing the in-game economy is essential for creating a fair, engaging, and sustainable game. By implementing fair pricing, robust reward systems, balanced progression, and data-driven decisions, developers can ensure that the economy enhances the player experience and supports long-term monetization. Continuous testing, updates, and community engagement are crucial for maintaining this balance and keeping players invested in the game.

4.5 Case Studies of Successful In-Game Purchase Strategies

Analyzing case studies of successful in-game purchase strategies can provide valuable insights into effective monetization techniques. Here are several examples of games that have excelled in this area, along with the strategies that contributed to their success.

1. **Fortnite**: Epic Games' "Fortnite" is a prime example of a successful in-game purchase strategy. The game offers a free-to-play battle royale mode with optional in-game purchases for cosmetic items such as skins, emotes, and back bling. Fortnite's success can be attributed to its frequent content updates, seasonal events, and the introduction of the Battle Pass. The Battle Pass offers exclusive rewards for completing challenges, creating a sense of progression and incentivizing players to spend money.
2. **Clash of Clans**: Supercell's "Clash of Clans" uses a freemium model with in-app purchases for in-game currency (gems), which can be used to speed up progression and purchase resources. The game's success lies in its balanced progression system, engaging gameplay, and regular content updates. Clan Wars and social features also encourage long-term engagement and spending.
3. **Candy Crush Saga**: King's "Candy Crush Saga" is a well-known example of effective in-game purchase strategies. The game offers a free-to-play experience with optional purchases for extra moves, lives, and boosters. Time-limited offers and special events create urgency and encourage spending. The game's simple yet addictive gameplay, combined with a fair progression system, has kept players engaged and willing to make in-game purchases.
4. **Pokémon GO**: Niantic's "Pokémon GO" integrates in-game purchases with real-world exploration. Players can buy items such as Poké Balls, incubators, and raid passes. The game's success is driven by its unique gameplay mechanics, regular community events, and updates that introduce new Pokémon and features. The combination of real-world engagement and in-game purchases has created a loyal and active player base.
5. **Genshin Impact**: miHoYo's "Genshin Impact" uses a gacha-based monetization system, where players spend in-game currency (primogems) to obtain random characters and weapons. The game's success is due to its high-quality graphics, engaging storyline, and frequent updates that introduce new content. The gacha system, while controversial, has proven effective in generating revenue by appealing to players' desire for rare and powerful items.
6. **PUBG Mobile**: Tencent's "PUBG Mobile" offers a free-to-play battle royale experience with in-game purchases for cosmetic items and the Royale Pass. The Royale Pass provides exclusive rewards for completing missions and progressing through tiers. The game's realistic graphics, competitive gameplay, and regular updates have contributed to its success and high revenue from in-game purchases.
7. **Hearthstone**: Blizzard's "Hearthstone" is a digital card game that monetizes through card pack purchases. Players can buy packs to expand their card collection and build competitive decks. The game's success is due to its engaging mechanics, regular expansions, and balance updates that keep the meta fresh. Special events and promotions also encourage spending on card packs.
8. **Roblox**: Roblox Corporation's "Roblox" allows users to create and share their own games within the platform. The game monetizes through the sale of Robux, the in-game currency used to purchase items, accessories, and game passes. The platform's success is driven by its user-generated content, social features, and regular events that promote spending and engagement.
9. **Among Us**: InnerSloth's "Among Us" offers a free-to-play experience with in-game purchases for cosmetic items such as hats, skins, and pets. The game's success is due to its simple yet engaging gameplay, social interaction, and the ability to

customize characters. Regular updates and community-driven content have kept players invested and willing to spend on cosmetics.
10. **League of Legends: Wild Rift**: Riot Games' "League of Legends: Wild Rift" monetizes through the sale of champions, skins, and in-game currency. The game's success is attributed to its competitive gameplay, regular updates, and the appeal of collecting and customizing champions. Seasonal events and limited-time offers also drive engagement and spending.

In conclusion, these case studies highlight various successful in-game purchase strategies. Key factors contributing to their success include regular content updates, balanced progression systems, engaging gameplay, and effective use of cosmetic and functional items. By analyzing these examples, developers can gain insights into creating compelling in-game purchase strategies that enhance player experience and drive revenue.

Chapter 5: Advertising in Mobile Games

5.1: Types of In-Game Advertising

In-game advertising has become a fundamental aspect of monetisation strategies for mobile games. Various types of in-game ads are employed to generate revenue while keeping the gaming experience engaging for players. Understanding these types helps in designing a balanced monetisation strategy.

Banner Ads

Banner ads are static or animated images displayed at the top or bottom of the screen during gameplay. They are non-intrusive but often overlooked by players due to banner blindness.

Interstitial Ads

Interstitial ads are full-screen advertisements that appear at natural transition points within the game, such as between levels. These ads are more engaging but can disrupt gameplay if not implemented carefully.

Rewarded Video Ads

Rewarded video ads offer players in-game rewards, such as extra lives or currency, in exchange for watching a short video. This type of ad is highly effective as it provides value to the player and ensures high completion rates.

Native Ads

Native ads blend seamlessly into the game's interface, matching the look and feel of the game. These ads are less disruptive and can enhance the overall user experience if done correctly.

Playable Ads

Playable ads allow players to interact with a mini-version of the advertised game. This hands-on experience increases engagement and provides a taste of the gameplay, potentially driving higher conversion rates.

Offerwalls

Offerwalls present players with a list of tasks, such as installing apps or completing surveys, in exchange for in-game rewards. This type of ad provides multiple engagement opportunities but may require careful integration to avoid disrupting the game flow.

Cross-Promotion

Cross-promotion involves advertising other games developed by the same company within the game. This strategy helps retain users within the developer's ecosystem and can be highly effective if the advertised games are similar in genre and appeal.

Sponsorships

Sponsorships involve collaboration with brands to create custom content or events within the game. This type of ad can provide significant revenue and enhance the player experience through unique and engaging content.

Audio Ads

Audio ads play during gameplay, typically during moments when visual ads would be disruptive. They offer a way to monetise without interrupting the visual flow of the game, although they must be balanced to avoid annoying players.

Social Media Ads

Integration with social media platforms allows for targeted advertising based on user data. These ads can appear as recommendations or promotions within the game and leverage social media's extensive reach.

Understanding these various types of in-game ads is crucial for developers aiming to maximise revenue while maintaining a positive player experience. The choice of ad type should align with the game's design and player expectations to ensure success.

5.2: Integrating Ads Without Disrupting Gameplay

Integrating advertisements into mobile games without disrupting gameplay is a delicate balance. Effective ad integration ensures that the monetisation strategy enhances rather than detracts from the player experience.

Contextual Placement

Ads should be placed at natural breakpoints in the game, such as between levels or after completing a mission. This reduces the likelihood of interrupting the player's immersion and maintains the game's flow.

Rewarded Ads as Incentives

Rewarded ads, where players voluntarily watch an ad in exchange for in-game rewards, are a popular method. These ads provide value to the player and encourage engagement without forcing interruptions.

Frequency Capping

Implementing frequency capping ensures that players are not bombarded with ads. Limiting the number of ads shown per session or per hour can prevent ad fatigue and maintain player satisfaction.

Customised Ad Experience

Customising ads based on player preferences and behavior can enhance the relevance and effectiveness of ads. Using data analytics to tailor ads ensures that players see content that interests them, improving engagement rates.

Native Advertising

Native ads, designed to match the look and feel of the game, can be integrated seamlessly into the gameplay experience. These ads are less intrusive and can provide a more cohesive experience for players.

Non-Interruptive Ad Formats

Using non-interruptive ad formats, such as banner ads or audio ads, can monetise without significantly disrupting gameplay. These formats allow players to continue their gaming experience with minimal distraction.

Transparent Communication

Clearly communicating the presence and purpose of ads can build trust with players. Explaining that ads help support the game's development and maintenance can foster a more accepting attitude towards them.

Balanced Ad-to-Content Ratio

Maintaining a balanced ratio of ads to content is essential. Overloading a game with ads can lead to negative player feedback and decreased retention. Ensuring that ads complement rather than dominate the gameplay is key.

User Testing and Feedback

Conducting user testing and gathering feedback on ad implementation can provide valuable insights. Players can offer perspectives on how ads impact their experience, allowing developers to make informed adjustments.

Flexible Ad Settings

Providing players with control over ad settings, such as opting in for more frequent ads in exchange for higher rewards, can enhance the player experience. This flexibility respects player preferences and can increase engagement.

Dynamic Ad Insertion

Using technology to dynamically insert ads at appropriate times based on player behavior and game progress can optimise the ad experience. This approach ensures that ads are shown when least likely to disrupt gameplay.

Integrating ads thoughtfully and strategically can enhance the monetisation potential of a mobile game while preserving a positive player experience. Balancing revenue generation with player satisfaction is the cornerstone of successful ad integration.

5.3: Revenue Models for In-Game Advertising

Revenue models for in-game advertising vary, each with its own advantages and challenges. Understanding these models is essential for developers to maximise earnings from their mobile games.

Cost Per Impression (CPM)

Cost Per Impression (CPM) is a model where advertisers pay for every thousand impressions their ad receives. This model is beneficial for games with high user engagement, as it generates steady revenue based on ad views.

Cost Per Click (CPC)

Cost Per Click (CPC) involves advertisers paying each time a player clicks on an ad. This model encourages higher engagement and interaction but requires ads to be compelling enough to entice clicks.

Cost Per Action (CPA)

Cost Per Action (CPA) is a performance-based model where advertisers pay when players complete a specific action, such as making a purchase or signing up for a service. This model can be highly lucrative but depends on the player's willingness to take the desired action.

Revenue Sharing

Revenue sharing involves splitting the ad revenue between the game developer and the ad network. This model aligns the interests of both parties and can incentivise higher ad performance.

Subscription-Based Ad Removal

Offering players the option to pay a subscription fee to remove ads from the game can generate steady revenue while enhancing the player experience. This model caters to players who prefer an ad-free experience.

Rewarded Ad Revenue

Rewarded ads provide players with in-game rewards for watching ads. This model encourages voluntary ad engagement and can lead to higher completion rates, increasing revenue.

In-App Purchases Combined with Ads

Combining in-app purchases with ads allows players to either purchase items directly or earn them through ad engagement. This hybrid approach can maximise revenue by catering to different player preferences.

Sponsorship Deals

Securing sponsorship deals with brands can provide substantial revenue. Sponsored content or events within the game can enhance the player experience while offering advertisers unique promotional opportunities.

Programmatic Advertising

Programmatic advertising uses automated systems to buy and place ads in real-time. This model can optimise ad placements based on data, improving relevance and revenue potential.

Direct Deals with Advertisers

Negotiating direct deals with advertisers can provide higher revenue rates and more control over ad content. This model requires more effort in securing partnerships but can be highly rewarding.

Ad Mediation Platforms

Using ad mediation platforms allows developers to manage multiple ad networks and optimise ad performance. These platforms can increase fill rates and revenue by dynamically selecting the best-performing ads.

Dynamic Pricing Models

Dynamic pricing models adjust ad prices based on demand and player engagement. This approach can maximise revenue by capitalising on peak times and high-engagement periods.

Choosing the right revenue model for in-game advertising depends on the game's design, player base, and monetisation strategy. Combining multiple models can diversify revenue streams and enhance overall earnings.

5.4: Measuring Ad Effectiveness

Measuring ad effectiveness is crucial to optimise in-game advertising strategies and maximise revenue. Effective measurement involves tracking various metrics and using analytical tools to assess ad performance.

Key Performance Indicators (KPIs)

Identifying and tracking key performance indicators (KPIs) is the first step in measuring ad effectiveness. Common KPIs include impressions, clicks, click-through rates (CTR), conversion rates, and revenue per impression.

Impressions

Impressions measure how often an ad is displayed. High impression counts indicate good visibility, but they must be balanced with engagement metrics to assess overall effectiveness.

Click-Through Rate (CTR)

Click-through rate (CTR) measures the percentage of players who click on an ad after seeing it. A high CTR indicates that the ad content is compelling and relevant to the audience.

Conversion Rate

Conversion rate tracks the percentage of players who complete a desired action after clicking on an ad. This metric is critical for performance-based models like CPA and provides insights into ad quality and targeting.

Revenue Per Impression (RPI)

Revenue per impression (RPI) calculates the average revenue generated per ad view. This metric helps assess the overall profitability of ad placements and can guide optimisation efforts.

Ad Viewability

Ad viewability measures whether an ad was actually seen by players. High viewability rates indicate effective ad placements, while low rates may suggest issues with ad visibility or placement.

Engagement Metrics

Engagement metrics, such as time spent viewing an ad or interaction rates with playable ads, provide insights into player interest and ad effectiveness. Higher engagement often correlates with better ad performance.

A/B Testing

A/B testing involves comparing different versions of an ad to determine which performs better. This method helps optimise ad content, placement, and targeting for maximum effectiveness.

Retention Impact

Measuring the impact of ads on player retention is essential. Ads that negatively affect retention can harm long-term revenue, so balancing ad frequency and content is crucial.

User Feedback

Collecting and analysing user feedback on ads provides qualitative insights into player experiences. Understanding player sentiments can guide adjustments to improve ad acceptance and effectiveness.

Return on Ad Spend (ROAS)

Return on ad spend (ROAS) calculates the revenue generated for every dollar spent on advertising. This metric helps assess the overall efficiency of ad campaigns and informs budget allocation decisions.

Analytics Tools

Using analytics tools, such as Google Analytics, Firebase, or custom dashboards, allows developers to track and analyse ad performance data in real-time. These tools provide detailed insights and support data-driven decision-making.

Heatmaps

Heatmaps visually represent where players interact most with ads, providing insights into optimal ad placement. This method helps identify high-engagement areas within the game interface.

Attribution Models

Attribution models track the player journey and attribute conversions to specific ads. This approach provides a holistic view of ad performance and helps optimise cross-channel advertising strategies.

Continuous Monitoring

Continuous monitoring and adjusting ad strategies based on real-time data ensures sustained ad effectiveness. Regularly reviewing metrics and making data-driven adjustments can significantly enhance ad performance.

Effective measurement of ad effectiveness involves a combination of quantitative metrics and qualitative insights. By continuously monitoring and optimising ad strategies, developers can maximise revenue while maintaining a positive player experience.

5.5: Challenges and Opportunities in Mobile Game Advertising

Mobile game advertising presents both challenges and opportunities for developers seeking to monetise their games. Navigating these factors effectively can lead to successful and sustainable monetisation strategies.

Challenge: Ad Fatigue

Ad fatigue occurs when players become overwhelmed by too many ads, leading to decreased engagement and potential churn. Balancing ad frequency and content is essential to avoid this issue.

Opportunity: Personalised Ads

Personalised ads tailored to individual player preferences and behaviors can significantly increase engagement and effectiveness. Leveraging data analytics to deliver relevant ads enhances the player experience and boosts revenue.

Challenge: Ad Blockers

The use of ad blockers can reduce the visibility of ads and impact revenue. Developing ad experiences that players find valuable and engaging can mitigate the use of ad blockers.

Opportunity: Rewarded Ads

Rewarded ads offer a mutually beneficial solution by providing players with in-game rewards in exchange for ad engagement. This approach increases ad viewability and player satisfaction.

Challenge: Maintaining Game Balance

Integrating ads without disrupting gameplay or altering game balance is a critical challenge. Thoughtful ad placement and design can ensure that ads complement rather than detract from the gaming experience.

Opportunity: Cross-Promotion

Cross-promotion within a developer's portfolio can drive user acquisition and retention. Promoting similar games to existing players can keep them within the developer's ecosystem and increase lifetime value.

Challenge: Regulatory Compliance

Adhering to privacy regulations and ensuring compliance with data protection laws is essential. Developers must navigate complex legal landscapes to avoid penalties and maintain player trust.

Opportunity: Sponsorships and Partnerships

Sponsorships and partnerships with brands can provide significant revenue opportunities. Collaborating on in-game events or custom content can enhance the player experience and offer unique promotional avenues.

Challenge: Measuring Ad Effectiveness

Accurately measuring ad effectiveness and attributing conversions to specific ads can be complex. Employing robust analytics tools and attribution models is crucial for informed decision-making.

Opportunity: Emerging Ad Formats

Emerging ad formats, such as augmented reality (AR) and virtual reality (VR) ads, offer innovative ways to engage players. Exploring these formats can provide a competitive edge and attract new audiences.

Challenge: Player Retention

Ensuring that ads do not negatively impact player retention is vital. Developers must balance monetisation efforts with maintaining a loyal player base to ensure long-term success.

Opportunity: Programmatic Advertising

Programmatic advertising automates the buying and placement of ads, optimising ad performance and revenue. Leveraging programmatic platforms can streamline ad management and improve results.

Challenge: Diverse Player Preferences

Catering to diverse player preferences and ensuring ads appeal to a broad audience can be challenging. Personalisation and segmentation strategies can help address this issue effectively.

Opportunity: In-Game Events

In-game events tied to ad campaigns can create engaging and memorable experiences for players. These events can drive higher engagement and provide unique advertising opportunities.

Challenge: Technical Integration

Integrating ads seamlessly into the game's code and ensuring compatibility across devices can be technically challenging. Collaborating with experienced ad networks and platforms can ease this process.

Opportunity: Data-Driven Optimisation

Utilising data-driven optimisation techniques can enhance ad performance. Continuous analysis and adjustment based on real-time data ensure that ad strategies remain effective and relevant.

Challenge: Maintaining Player Trust

Overly aggressive or intrusive ads can erode player trust and lead to negative feedback. Transparent communication and ethical ad practices are essential to maintaining a positive player relationship.

Opportunity: Expanding Global Markets

Expanding into global markets with tailored ad strategies can unlock new revenue streams. Understanding regional preferences and cultural differences is key to successful global advertising campaigns.

Challenge: Ad Fraud

Ad fraud, such as fake clicks and impressions, can distort performance metrics and impact revenue. Implementing robust fraud detection and prevention measures is crucial to safeguarding ad revenue.

Opportunity: Continuous Innovation

Continuously innovating and experimenting with new ad formats and strategies can keep the ad experience fresh and engaging for players. Staying ahead of trends ensures sustained monetisation success.

Navigating the challenges and opportunities in mobile game advertising requires a strategic approach and a deep understanding of player preferences. By leveraging opportunities and addressing challenges effectively, developers can achieve successful and sustainable monetisation.

Chapter 6: Player Retention and Engagement

6.1: Importance of Retention for Monetisation

Player retention is a critical factor in the success of mobile game monetisation strategies. High retention rates indicate that players are engaged and satisfied with the game, which directly impacts revenue generation and long-term profitability.

Long-Term Revenue

Retaining players over the long term increases their lifetime value (LTV). Players who stay engaged with the game are more likely to make repeated in-app purchases and interact with ads, driving consistent revenue.

Word-of-Mouth Promotion

Satisfied players are more likely to recommend the game to friends and family, leading to organic growth through word-of-mouth promotion. High retention rates can thus indirectly contribute to user acquisition.

Cost Efficiency

Acquiring new users is often more expensive than retaining existing ones. By focusing on retention, developers can reduce marketing costs and allocate resources more efficiently towards enhancing the player experience.

Enhancing Player Experience

A focus on retention encourages developers to continuously improve the game. Regular updates, new content, and addressing player feedback help keep the game fresh and engaging, fostering long-term loyalty.

Building a Community

High retention rates facilitate the growth of a strong player community. Active communities enhance the gaming experience through social interactions, support, and shared experiences, contributing to player satisfaction and retention.

Maximising Ad Revenue

Retained players are more likely to engage with in-game ads, increasing ad impressions and clicks. A stable and engaged player base provides a reliable source of ad revenue for developers.

Data-Driven Insights

Long-term players generate valuable data that can be used to refine and optimise monetisation strategies. Understanding player behavior and preferences helps in making informed decisions that enhance retention and revenue.

Competitive Advantage

High retention rates can give a game a competitive edge in the crowded mobile gaming market. Games that retain players well are more likely to be featured and recommended by app stores, increasing visibility and downloads.

Predictable Revenue Streams

With high retention rates, developers can predict revenue streams more accurately. This predictability aids in financial planning and investment decisions, ensuring the sustainability of the game.

Reducing Churn

Focusing on retention helps identify and address factors contributing to player churn. By understanding why players leave and implementing measures to mitigate these issues, developers can maintain a stable player base.

Leveraging In-Game Events

Regular in-game events and promotions tailored to long-term players can boost engagement and retention. These events create excitement and provide incentives for players to continue playing.

Personalised Experiences

Personalising the gaming experience based on player data enhances retention. Tailored content, rewards, and recommendations make players feel valued and understood, increasing their loyalty to the game.

Feedback Loop

Engaged players provide valuable feedback that can be used to improve the game. Establishing a feedback loop where player input is actively sought and implemented helps build a loyal player base.

Cross-Promotion Opportunities

A retained player base is more receptive to cross-promotion of other games developed by the same company. This strategy helps retain users within the developer's ecosystem and increases overall revenue.

Ethical Monetisation

High retention rates allow for more ethical monetisation practices. Developers can focus on providing value and enhancing the player experience rather than relying on aggressive monetisation tactics that may alienate players.

Community-Driven Content

Encouraging user-generated content and community involvement can boost retention. Players who feel a sense of ownership and contribution to the game are more likely to stay engaged.

Maintaining Balance

Balancing game difficulty and reward systems to cater to different player skill levels helps in retaining a diverse player base. Ensuring that both casual and hardcore players find the game enjoyable is key to high retention.

Real-Time Analytics

Utilising real-time analytics to monitor player behavior and engagement allows for timely interventions. Identifying and addressing issues as they arise helps maintain high retention rates.

Continuous Improvement

A commitment to continuous improvement and innovation keeps the game relevant and exciting. Regular updates and new features show players that the developers are invested in their experience.

Monetisation Opportunities

Retained players provide more opportunities for monetisation through in-app purchases, subscriptions, and ads. A loyal player base is more likely to spend money and engage with monetisation elements.

Focusing on player retention is crucial for the success of mobile game monetisation. High retention rates lead to increased revenue, reduced costs, and a strong community, ensuring the long-term sustainability of the game.

6.2: Strategies for Increasing Player Retention

Increasing player retention requires a multifaceted approach that addresses various aspects of the gaming experience. Implementing effective strategies can significantly enhance player engagement and loyalty.

Onboarding Experience

A smooth and engaging onboarding experience helps new players understand the game mechanics quickly. Providing tutorials, tips, and a gradual learning curve ensures that players do not feel overwhelmed and are more likely to continue playing.

Regular Updates and Content

Frequent updates and new content keep the game fresh and exciting. Adding new levels, characters, events, and features encourages players to return and explore the latest additions.

Personalised Content

Tailoring content based on player preferences and behavior enhances the gaming experience. Personalised recommendations, rewards, and challenges make players feel valued and understood, increasing their loyalty.

Reward Systems

Implementing robust reward systems that offer meaningful incentives keeps players motivated. Daily rewards, achievement badges, and special event prizes encourage players to log in regularly and strive for new goals.

Social Features

Integrating social features such as friend lists, multiplayer modes, and social media sharing fosters a sense of community. Players who can connect and compete with friends are more likely to stay engaged.

Gamification Techniques

Applying gamification techniques, such as leaderboards, quests, and missions, adds an extra layer of engagement. These elements create a sense of achievement and progression, motivating players to continue playing.

Responsive Support

Providing responsive and helpful customer support builds trust with players. Addressing issues, answering questions, and showing that player feedback is valued enhances the overall experience and retention.

In-Game Events

Organising regular in-game events, such as tournaments, holiday-themed activities, and special challenges, generates excitement. These events provide unique opportunities for players to earn exclusive rewards and engage with the game.

Balancing Difficulty

Ensuring that the game's difficulty is balanced for different skill levels is crucial. Offering adjustable difficulty settings or adaptive challenges helps cater to both casual and hardcore players, preventing frustration and dropout.

Clear Progression Paths

Designing clear progression paths with achievable milestones keeps players motivated. Providing a sense of direction and purpose encourages players to invest more time in the game.

Community Engagement

Engaging with the player community through forums, social media, and in-game chat fosters a sense of belonging. Active communities enhance the gaming experience through shared tips, support, and camaraderie.

Cross-Promotion

Cross-promoting within the developer's portfolio of games can retain players within the ecosystem. Offering rewards or incentives for trying other games by the same developer helps maintain player interest.

Feedback Integration

Actively seeking and integrating player feedback into game updates shows that the developers value player input. This approach builds trust and loyalty, as players feel their voices are heard and their suggestions implemented.

Seamless UX

Ensuring a seamless user experience with intuitive controls, smooth navigation, and minimal loading times enhances player satisfaction. A polished and user-friendly interface keeps players engaged and reduces frustration.

Monetisation Balance

Balancing monetisation elements with gameplay is essential. Avoiding aggressive or intrusive monetisation practices ensures that players do not feel pressured or exploited, enhancing retention.

Player Segmentation

Segmenting players based on their behavior and preferences allows for targeted engagement strategies. Customising offers, challenges, and content for different player segments ensures that each group feels catered to.

In-Game Personalisation

Offering in-game personalisation options, such as custom avatars, skins, and items, enhances the player experience. Allowing players to express themselves and customise their gaming environment fosters a deeper connection with the game.

Real-Time Analytics

Utilising real-time analytics to monitor player behavior and engagement provides valuable insights. Identifying patterns and trends helps in making data-driven decisions to enhance retention strategies.

Collaborative Play

Introducing collaborative play elements, such as team challenges and cooperative missions, encourages social interaction. Players who can work together and support each other are more likely to remain engaged.

Transparent Communication

Maintaining transparent communication with players about updates, changes, and future plans builds trust. Keeping players informed and involved in the game's development fosters a sense of ownership and loyalty.

Implementing these strategies can significantly enhance player retention and ensure the long-term success of a mobile game. By focusing on player engagement, satisfaction, and loyalty, developers can create a sustainable and profitable gaming experience.

6.3: Gamification and Engagement Techniques

Gamification involves incorporating game-like elements into non-game contexts to enhance engagement and motivation. In mobile games, gamification techniques can significantly increase player retention and satisfaction.

Achievement Systems

Implementing achievement systems that reward players for completing specific tasks or reaching milestones adds a sense of accomplishment. These rewards can be in the form of badges, trophies, or in-game currency.

Leaderboards

Leaderboards create a competitive environment by ranking players based on their performance. Seeing their name on a leaderboard motivates players to improve and achieve higher rankings.

Daily Challenges

Daily challenges provide short-term goals that encourage players to log in and play regularly. These challenges can vary in difficulty and offer rewards upon completion, maintaining player interest.

Quests and Missions

Quests and missions add a narrative element to the game, providing players with clear objectives and a sense of purpose. Completing these tasks often leads to rewards and progression within the game.

Progress Bars

Displaying progress bars for tasks or goals helps players visualize their advancement. Seeing their progress motivates players to continue playing to reach the next milestone.

Customisation Options

Allowing players to customise their avatars, environments, and items adds a personal touch to the game. Customisation options enable players to express themselves and feel more connected to the game.

Social Sharing

Integrating social sharing features enables players to share their achievements, high scores, and progress with friends on social media. This fosters a sense of pride and encourages others to join the game.

In-Game Events

Hosting regular in-game events, such as tournaments and special challenges, creates excitement and anticipation. These events provide unique rewards and experiences, keeping players engaged.

Virtual Economies

Creating a virtual economy with in-game currency and items adds depth to the game. Players can earn, trade, and spend currency on various items, enhancing their overall experience.

Feedback Systems

Implementing feedback systems, such as ratings and reviews, allows players to provide input on the game. Developers can use this feedback to make improvements and show players that their opinions are valued.

Time-Limited Rewards

Offering time-limited rewards, such as exclusive items or bonuses, creates a sense of urgency. Players are motivated to log in and play during specific periods to earn these rewards.

Collaborative Play

Encouraging collaborative play through team challenges, guilds, or co-op missions fosters social interaction. Players who can work together and support each other are more likely to remain engaged.

Narrative Elements

Incorporating narrative elements and storytelling enhances the immersive experience. A compelling storyline keeps players invested in the game's world and characters.

Interactive Tutorials

Interactive tutorials that guide new players through the game mechanics ensure a smooth onboarding experience. Well-designed tutorials help players understand the game quickly and reduce the risk of early dropout.

Adaptive Difficulty

Implementing adaptive difficulty levels that adjust based on player performance ensures that the game remains challenging yet enjoyable. This balance prevents frustration and maintains player interest.

Rewards for Loyalty

Rewarding long-term players with exclusive bonuses, items, or privileges encourages loyalty. Recognising and valuing loyal players fosters a positive relationship and enhances retention.

Dynamic Content

Regularly updating the game with new content, such as levels, characters, and features, keeps the experience fresh. Dynamic content ensures that players always have something new to explore.

Mini-Games

Including mini-games within the main game provides variety and breaks the monotony. Mini-games offer different gameplay experiences and can be used as a form of relaxation or challenge.

Interactive Elements

Adding interactive elements, such as puzzles, hidden objects, and decision-making scenarios, enhances engagement. These elements require active participation and keep players mentally stimulated.

In-Game Analytics

Utilising in-game analytics to track player behavior and preferences helps developers refine gamification techniques. Understanding what engages players allows for targeted improvements and optimised experiences.

Gamification techniques enhance player engagement and retention by providing structure, motivation, and rewards. By incorporating these elements into mobile games, developers can create compelling and enjoyable experiences that keep players coming back.

6.4: Community Building and Social Features

Community building and social features play a crucial role in enhancing player retention and engagement in mobile games. Creating a vibrant and active community fosters a sense of belonging and encourages long-term loyalty.

Social Interactions

Enabling social interactions, such as chat systems, friend lists, and in-game messaging, allows players to connect and communicate. These features create a sense of camaraderie and support among players.

Multiplayer Modes

Introducing multiplayer modes where players can team up or compete against each other enhances the social experience. Cooperative and competitive gameplay fosters relationships and keeps players engaged.

Guilds and Clans

Forming guilds or clans provides players with a structured social group. Guilds offer shared goals, collaborative challenges, and exclusive rewards, creating a strong sense of community.

Community Events

Hosting community events, such as tournaments, contests, and live streams, generates excitement and participation. These events bring players together and provide opportunities for social interaction.

User-Generated Content

Encouraging user-generated content, such as custom levels, skins, and mods, allows players to contribute to the game. This involvement fosters creativity and a sense of ownership within the community.

Social Media Integration

Integrating social media features enables players to share their achievements, progress, and experiences with friends. Social media platforms also serve as a channel for community engagement and promotion.

Leaderboards and Rankings

Displaying leaderboards and rankings publicly fosters healthy competition and recognition. Players strive to achieve higher rankings, which can be shared and celebrated within the community.

Community Forums

Establishing community forums or discussion boards provides a space for players to share tips, strategies, and experiences. Forums facilitate knowledge sharing and strengthen the community bond.

Developer Interaction

Active interaction between developers and players, such as responding to feedback, hosting Q&A sessions, and sharing updates, builds trust. Players feel valued and heard, enhancing their connection to the game.

In-Game Avatars and Profiles

Allowing players to create and customise in-game avatars and profiles adds a personal touch. Avatars and profiles serve as a representation of the player within the community.

Collaborative Challenges

Introducing collaborative challenges that require teamwork fosters cooperation and social interaction. Players working together towards a common goal strengthens community ties.

Virtual Events and Celebrations

Hosting virtual events and celebrations, such as holiday-themed activities and anniversaries, creates a festive atmosphere. These events provide unique experiences and rewards, enhancing player engagement.

Player Recognition

Recognising and celebrating player achievements, such as top scorers, long-term players, and community contributors, fosters a positive environment. Recognition motivates players to remain active and engaged.

In-Game Surveys and Polls

Conducting in-game surveys and polls allows players to voice their opinions and preferences. This involvement in decision-making processes makes players feel valued and connected.

Mentorship Programs

Implementing mentorship programs where experienced players guide newcomers fosters a supportive community. Mentors help new players acclimate, enhancing their initial experience and retention.

Community Guidelines

Establishing clear community guidelines ensures a respectful and inclusive environment. Enforcing these guidelines maintains a positive atmosphere where players feel safe and welcome.

Cross-Platform Play

Enabling cross-platform play allows players to connect and compete with friends regardless of the device they use. Cross-platform compatibility broadens the community and enhances social interactions.

Feedback Loops

Creating feedback loops where player input directly influences game updates and features builds a collaborative relationship. Players feel a sense of contribution and ownership, enhancing their loyalty.

In-Game Community Spaces

Designing in-game community spaces, such as lounges or hubs, where players can gather and interact enhances social engagement. These spaces provide a focal point for community activities and interactions.

Building a strong community and integrating social features into mobile games fosters player retention and engagement. A vibrant community enhances the overall gaming experience, creating a sense of belonging and encouraging long-term loyalty.

6.5: Analysing Retention Metrics

Analysing retention metrics is essential for understanding player behavior and optimising strategies to enhance retention. Effective analysis provides insights into what keeps players engaged and identifies areas for improvement.

Key Retention Metrics

Identifying and tracking key retention metrics, such as Day 1, Day 7, and Day 30 retention rates, provides a snapshot of player retention over time. These metrics help assess the initial and long-term engagement of players.

Cohort Analysis

Cohort analysis involves grouping players based on shared characteristics or behaviors and tracking their retention over time. This method provides insights into how different segments of players engage with the game.

Churn Rate

Churn rate measures the percentage of players who stop playing the game over a specific period. Understanding churn helps identify factors that contribute to player dropout and develop strategies to reduce it.

Lifetime Value (LTV)

Lifetime value (LTV) calculates the total revenue generated by a player over their lifetime in the game. Higher retention rates contribute to increased LTV, making it a crucial metric for assessing long-term success.

Session Length

Tracking session length provides insights into how long players engage with the game during each play session. Longer sessions often indicate higher engagement and satisfaction.

Session Frequency

Session frequency measures how often players return to the game within a specific period. High session frequency suggests strong player engagement and habit formation.

Active Users

Monitoring daily active users (DAU) and monthly active users (MAU) provides an overview of the game's active player base. A healthy balance between DAU and MAU indicates sustained engagement.

Stickiness Ratio

The stickiness ratio, calculated as DAU/MAU, measures the percentage of monthly users who play the game daily. A high stickiness ratio indicates strong player loyalty and engagement.

In-Game Events Participation

Tracking participation in in-game events provides insights into what activities and rewards resonate with players. High participation rates suggest successful event design and engagement.

Time to First Purchase

Time to first purchase measures the duration between a player's first session and their first in-app purchase. Shorter times to first purchase indicate effective monetisation strategies and player satisfaction.

Player Feedback

Collecting and analysing player feedback through surveys, reviews, and in-game comments provides qualitative insights into player satisfaction and areas for improvement.

A/B Testing

Conducting A/B testing on different game elements, such as tutorials, features, and monetisation options, helps identify what resonates best with players. This method supports data-driven decision-making.

Heatmaps

Using heatmaps to visualise player interactions within the game provides insights into popular and problematic areas. Heatmaps help optimise game design and improve the player experience.

Funnel Analysis

Funnel analysis tracks the player journey through different stages of the game, from onboarding to advanced levels. Identifying drop-off points within the funnel helps address issues and improve retention.

Social Engagement

Monitoring social engagement metrics, such as friend invites, multiplayer participation, and social media shares, provides insights into the effectiveness of social features in driving retention.

Player Segmentation

Segmenting players based on demographics, behavior, and spending patterns allows for targeted retention strategies. Personalised approaches for different segments enhance player satisfaction and loyalty.

Real-Time Analytics

Utilising real-time analytics to monitor player behavior and engagement provides immediate insights. Real-time data helps identify trends and issues as they arise, enabling timely interventions.

Retention Curves

Plotting retention curves over time provides a visual representation of player retention. Retention curves help identify critical drop-off points and assess the impact of changes on retention rates.

Benchmarking

Comparing retention metrics against industry benchmarks and competitor data provides context for assessing performance. Benchmarking helps set realistic goals and identify areas for improvement.

Predictive Analytics

Using predictive analytics to forecast player behavior and retention trends supports proactive strategy development. Predictive models help anticipate challenges and opportunities in retention.

Continuous Monitoring

Implementing continuous monitoring of retention metrics ensures that data is always up-to-date. Regular reviews and adjustments based on data insights keep retention strategies effective.

Effective analysis of retention metrics provides a comprehensive understanding of player behavior and engagement. By leveraging these insights, developers can optimise strategies to enhance retention and ensure the long-term success of their mobile games.

Chapter 7: Designing Monetisation-Friendly Game Mechanics

7.1 Game Design Principles for Monetisation

Designing monetisation-friendly game mechanics involves integrating revenue-generating elements seamlessly into the gameplay experience. This process requires a deep understanding of player psychology, game balance, and market trends.

A key principle in designing monetisation-friendly game mechanics is to ensure that the monetisation methods do not disrupt the player's enjoyment. Players should feel that spending money enhances their experience rather than being necessary to progress. This can be achieved by offering cosmetic items, time-saving options, and other non-essential purchases that add value without being intrusive.

Another important aspect is to create a sense of progression and reward. Players are more likely to spend money if they feel they are making tangible progress. This can be done through well-designed leveling systems, unlockable content, and regular updates that keep the game fresh and engaging.

Balancing the game economy is crucial. In-game currency should be plentiful enough that players can enjoy the game without spending real money, but scarce enough that purchasing currency provides a significant advantage. This balance can be maintained through careful analysis of player behavior and spending patterns.

Reward systems are also vital in monetisation-friendly game design. Implementing daily rewards, achievements, and special events encourages players to return regularly and invest more time (and money) into the game. These systems should be designed to create a loop of engagement and reward.

Integrating social features can enhance monetisation. Players are more likely to spend money on items that can be shown off to friends or that enhance their social status within the game. Features like leaderboards, clans, and social sharing options can boost both engagement and monetisation.

Testing and iteration are fundamental to refining monetisation strategies. Developers should continuously test different monetisation techniques, gather player feedback, and make adjustments based on data. A/B testing, where two versions of a feature are tested simultaneously, can provide valuable insights into player preferences and spending behavior.

Aesthetic appeal is another factor that can drive monetisation. High-quality graphics, engaging sound design, and a cohesive art style can enhance the perceived value of in-game purchases. Players are more likely to spend money in a game that looks and sounds appealing.

Transparency in monetisation practices is essential. Players should always know what they are paying for and feel that they are getting good value for their money. Hidden costs or manipulative tactics can lead to player dissatisfaction and damage the game's reputation.

Finally, ethical considerations should guide the design of monetisation mechanics. Exploiting players, especially vulnerable groups like children, can lead to negative consequences both legally and ethically. Developers should aim for fair monetisation practices that respect the player's investment of time and money.

In summary, designing monetisation-friendly game mechanics involves a careful balance of enhancing player experience, providing value, maintaining ethical standards, and continuously testing and iterating based on player feedback and data analysis.

7.2 Balancing Fun and Profit

Balancing fun and profit in mobile games is a delicate art that requires a deep understanding of both game design and player psychology. The goal is to create a game that is enjoyable and engaging while also being profitable for the developers.

The first step in achieving this balance is to ensure that the core gameplay is inherently fun. Players should enjoy the game itself, independent of any monetisation features. A game that relies too heavily on monetisation can quickly become frustrating and lose its player base. The core mechanics should be engaging, challenging, and rewarding on their own merits.

One effective strategy is to design monetisation features that complement the gameplay rather than interrupt it. For example, offering cosmetic items that allow players to customize their characters can enhance the fun without impacting the core gameplay. These items can be sold as in-app purchases or rewarded for completing certain in-game achievements.

Another approach is to provide time-saving options for players who want to progress faster. For instance, players might be able to purchase experience boosters or speed up building times. This allows players with less time to enjoy the game at their own pace while keeping the core mechanics intact for those who prefer not to spend money.

Balancing the in-game economy is crucial for maintaining both fun and profitability. In-game currency should be earnable through regular gameplay, but purchasing additional currency should provide a meaningful advantage. The key is to find a balance where players feel they can progress without spending money but are tempted to make purchases for convenience or faster progress.

Engagement loops are essential for keeping players invested in the game. Daily rewards, special events, and achievements can create a cycle of engagement that encourages players to return regularly. These features can also be tied to monetisation, such as offering special items or discounts during events.

Social features can enhance both fun and profit. Players are more likely to spend money on items that improve their social standing or allow them to interact more effectively with friends. Features like clans, leaderboards, and cooperative gameplay can boost engagement and provide opportunities for monetisation.

It's also important to regularly update the game with new content. This keeps the game fresh and exciting for players and provides new opportunities for monetisation. New levels, characters, and items can attract both new and returning players and encourage additional spending.

Transparency and fairness are key to maintaining player trust. Players should always know what they are getting when they spend money and feel that the prices are reasonable. Hidden costs or manipulative tactics can lead to player dissatisfaction and harm the game's reputation.

Ethical considerations are also important. Monetisation should never exploit players, especially vulnerable groups like children. Developers should aim for practices that are fair and respectful of the player's time and money.

In conclusion, balancing fun and profit in mobile games requires a careful blend of engaging gameplay, complementary monetisation features, fair pricing, and ethical practices. By focusing on creating a fun and rewarding experience for players, developers can achieve long-term profitability and success.

7.3 Reward Systems and Player Motivation

Reward systems are a fundamental aspect of game design that directly influence player motivation and engagement. Effective reward systems can drive player retention, encourage spending, and enhance the overall gaming experience.

At the core of any reward system is the principle of positive reinforcement. Players are more likely to continue playing and investing in a game if they feel that their actions are being rewarded. This can be achieved through various mechanisms, such as points, achievements, and in-game currency.

One of the most common types of reward systems is the leveling system. As players progress through the game, they earn experience points that contribute to their level. Each new level can unlock new abilities, items, or game content, providing a sense of progression and accomplishment.

Daily rewards are another effective tool for maintaining player engagement. By offering small rewards for logging in each day, developers can encourage players to make the game a part of their daily routine. These rewards can include in-game currency, items, or special bonuses.

Achievement systems also play a crucial role in motivating players. By setting specific goals or challenges, developers can provide players with clear objectives to strive for.

Achievements can range from simple tasks, like collecting a certain number of items, to more complex challenges, like completing a level without taking damage.

Event-based rewards can create excitement and drive player engagement. Special events, such as holiday-themed content or limited-time challenges, can offer unique rewards that are not available through regular gameplay. These events can also encourage players to spend money on special items or bundles.

Monetary rewards, such as in-game currency or premium items, can incentivize spending. Players are more likely to make purchases if they feel that they are getting good value for their money. Offering discounts, bundles, or limited-time offers can create a sense of urgency and encourage spending.

Social rewards can enhance the gaming experience by leveraging the social aspects of gameplay. Features like leaderboards, clans, and cooperative missions can provide players with a sense of community and competition. Social rewards, such as exclusive items or bonuses for top performers, can motivate players to engage more deeply with the game.

Random rewards, such as loot boxes or gacha mechanics, can create excitement and anticipation. However, these systems must be carefully balanced to avoid player frustration or perceptions of unfairness. Transparency and fairness are crucial to maintaining player trust in random reward systems.

Feedback loops are essential for keeping players engaged. By providing immediate and meaningful feedback for player actions, developers can reinforce desired behaviors and keep players motivated. This can include visual effects, sound cues, and progress bars that show how close players are to their next reward.

Data analytics can play a significant role in optimizing reward systems. By analyzing player behavior and preferences, developers can tailor rewards to better match player motivations. A/B testing can also be used to experiment with different reward structures and determine which ones are most effective.

In summary, reward systems are a powerful tool for driving player motivation and engagement. By offering meaningful and varied rewards, developers can create a compelling gameplay experience that encourages players to invest time and money into the game.

7.4 Integrating Monetisation into Game Narrative

Integrating monetisation into the game narrative is a strategy that can enhance player immersion and increase revenue without disrupting the gameplay experience. This approach involves weaving monetisation elements seamlessly into the storyline, characters, and world of the game.

A key principle in integrating monetisation into the game narrative is to ensure that these elements feel natural and cohesive. Players should feel that the opportunity to spend money enhances their experience rather than detracting from it. This can be achieved by designing monetisation features that are consistent with the game's lore and themes.

For example, in a fantasy game, players might have the opportunity to purchase magical items or potions that fit naturally into the game's world. These items can be presented as rare and valuable treasures that enhance the player's abilities or provide unique advantages.

Another effective strategy is to incorporate monetisation into character development. Players are often emotionally invested in their characters and are willing to spend money to customize and enhance them. Offering cosmetic items, special abilities, or exclusive outfits that align with the character's story can drive monetisation while deepening the player's connection to the game.

Quests and missions can also be designed to include monetisation opportunities. Special quests that offer unique rewards or access to premium content can encourage players to spend money. These quests should be integrated into the main storyline and provide meaningful benefits that enhance the player's experience.

Narrative-driven events can create excitement and drive player engagement. Limited-time events that introduce new storylines, characters, or challenges can offer exclusive rewards that are available for purchase. These events should be designed to feel like natural extensions of the game's narrative rather than standalone monetisation tactics.

Dialogue and character interactions can subtly promote monetisation. Characters within the game can reference special items, abilities, or upgrades that are available for purchase. These references should be woven into the dialogue in a way that feels organic and adds to the player's immersion in the game world.

Environmental storytelling can also support monetisation. In-game locations, such as shops, markets, or treasure chests, can offer opportunities for players to spend money. These locations should be designed to fit seamlessly into the game's world and provide a sense of discovery and excitement.

Feedback from players is crucial in refining the integration of monetisation into the game narrative. Developers should gather player feedback on how these elements impact their experience and make adjustments based on this input. Transparency and responsiveness to player concerns can help maintain trust and satisfaction.

Ethical considerations are important when integrating monetisation into the game narrative. Players should never feel forced to spend money to enjoy the game or progress through the story. Monetisation opportunities should enhance the experience and provide value without exploiting the player's investment.

In summary, integrating monetisation into the game narrative involves designing revenue-generating elements that enhance the player's immersion and enjoyment. By weaving these elements naturally into the storyline, characters, and world of the game, developers can create a cohesive and compelling experience that encourages players to invest both their time and money.

7.5 Testing and Iterating Monetisation Mechanics

Testing and iterating monetisation mechanics is a critical process in developing successful mobile games. This approach involves continuously evaluating and refining monetisation strategies based on player feedback and data analysis.

The first step in this process is to establish clear goals and metrics for monetisation. Developers should define what success looks like in terms of revenue, player engagement, and satisfaction. Key metrics might include average revenue per user (ARPU), conversion rates, and retention rates.

A/B testing is a valuable tool for testing monetisation mechanics. This method involves creating two or more versions of a feature and comparing their performance. For example, developers might test different pricing strategies, reward structures, or user interface designs to see which one generates the most revenue or engagement.

Player feedback is essential in the iteration process. Developers should actively seek feedback from players through surveys, focus groups, and in-game feedback tools. This feedback can provide valuable insights into what players like and dislike about the monetisation mechanics.

Data analytics plays a crucial role in understanding player behavior and preferences. By analyzing data on how players interact with the game and its monetisation features, developers can identify patterns and trends. This information can inform decisions about what to keep, change, or remove.

Iterating on monetisation mechanics involves making small, incremental changes rather than overhauling the entire system. This approach allows developers to test the impact of each change and avoid disrupting the overall game experience. For example, adjusting the price of an in-game item or altering the frequency of special offers can provide insights into player sensitivity to pricing.

Transparency with players is important when testing and iterating monetisation mechanics. Players should be informed about changes and the reasons behind them. This transparency helps build trust and reduces the risk of backlash from the player community.

Developers should also consider the long-term implications of monetisation changes. Short-term revenue boosts should not come at the expense of long-term player satisfaction and retention. Balancing immediate financial goals with the overall health of the game is crucial for sustainable success.

Ethical considerations are paramount in the testing and iteration process. Developers should avoid manipulative or exploitative practices that can harm players or damage the game's reputation. Fairness and respect for the player's investment of time and money should guide all decisions.

Continuous learning and adaptation are key to successful monetisation. The gaming industry is dynamic, with player preferences and market trends constantly evolving. Developers should stay informed about industry best practices, emerging technologies, and new monetisation models to keep their games competitive.

In conclusion, testing and iterating monetisation mechanics is a continuous process that involves setting clear goals, gathering player feedback, analyzing data, and making incremental changes. By focusing on player satisfaction and ethical practices, developers can create monetisation strategies that are both profitable and enjoyable for players.

Chapter 8: User Experience and Monetisation

8.1 Understanding Player Personas

Understanding player personas is a crucial aspect of designing effective monetisation strategies. Player personas represent different segments of the player base, each with unique characteristics, preferences, and spending behaviors.

The first step in developing player personas is to gather data on the player base. This can include demographic information, such as age, gender, and location, as well as psychographic data, such as interests, motivations, and gaming habits. Surveys, in-game analytics, and social media analysis can provide valuable insights into the player base.

Once data is collected, it can be used to identify distinct player segments. For example, some players might be highly competitive and motivated by achievements, while others might be more interested in social interactions and customization options. These segments can be used to create detailed player personas that represent the different types of players.

Each player persona should include information about the player's goals, preferences, and challenges. For example, a competitive player might be motivated by leaderboards and exclusive rewards, while a social player might value cooperative gameplay and customization options. Understanding these motivations can help developers design monetisation features that appeal to different segments of the player base.

Personalization is a powerful tool in monetisation. By tailoring offers and content to specific player personas, developers can increase the likelihood of engagement and spending. For example, a competitive player might be offered exclusive items that enhance their performance, while a social player might be offered special customization options.

Communication is also important in reaching different player personas. Different segments of the player base might respond to different types of messaging and marketing. For example, competitive players might be motivated by messages about exclusive rewards and achievements, while social players might respond to messages about community events and social features.

Testing and iteration are essential in refining player personas and monetisation strategies. By continuously gathering data and feedback, developers can refine their understanding of the player base and make adjustments to better meet their needs. A/B testing can be used to experiment with different approaches and determine which ones are most effective for different segments.

Ethical considerations should guide the use of player personas in monetisation. Developers should avoid exploiting players or using manipulative tactics to drive spending. Fairness and respect for the player's experience should be the guiding principles in designing monetisation strategies.

In summary, understanding player personas is a key aspect of designing effective monetisation strategies. By gathering data, identifying distinct segments, and tailoring offers and communication to different player types, developers can create a more engaging and profitable gaming experience.

8.2 UX Design Principles for Monetisation

UX design principles are critical in creating monetisation features that are both effective and user-friendly. Good UX design ensures that monetisation features enhance the player experience rather than detracting from it.

The first principle is to ensure that monetisation features are easy to find and use. Players should be able to access in-game stores, purchase items, and complete transactions without unnecessary steps or confusion. Clear navigation and intuitive interfaces are essential.

Consistency is another important principle. The design of monetisation features should be consistent with the overall look and feel of the game. This includes using the same visual style, typography, and color schemes. Consistency helps create a seamless experience and reinforces the game's brand.

Feedback is crucial in UX design for monetisation. Players should receive immediate and clear feedback when they make a purchase or interact with monetisation features. This can include visual and audio cues, confirmation messages, and progress indicators. Feedback helps reassure players that their actions have been successful and enhances their sense of accomplishment.

Transparency is key to building trust with players. Players should always know what they are getting when they spend money and how much it will cost. Hidden fees, ambiguous offers, and unclear terms can lead to frustration and distrust. Clear and honest communication about prices, offers, and rewards is essential.

Personalization can enhance the UX of monetisation features. By tailoring offers and content to individual players based on their behavior and preferences, developers can create a more engaging and relevant experience. Personalized recommendations, special offers, and targeted messages can increase the likelihood of engagement and spending.

Reducing friction is important in creating a smooth and enjoyable experience. Players should be able to make purchases quickly and easily without unnecessary barriers. This includes optimizing payment processes, minimizing loading times, and providing multiple payment options. Reducing friction helps prevent drop-offs and enhances the overall experience.

Ethical considerations are also important in UX design for monetisation. Developers should avoid using manipulative tactics that exploit players or create undue pressure to spend money. Fairness, transparency, and respect for the player's experience should guide all design decisions.

Testing and iteration are essential in refining UX design for monetisation. Developers should continuously gather data and feedback on how players interact with monetisation features and make adjustments based on this information. A/B testing can be used to experiment with different designs and determine which ones are most effective.

In summary, UX design principles are critical in creating monetisation features that enhance the player experience. By focusing on ease of use, consistency, feedback, transparency, personalization, and ethical considerations, developers can create a more engaging and profitable gaming experience.

8.3 Ensuring a Seamless Purchase Experience

Ensuring a seamless purchase experience is crucial for maximizing revenue and maintaining player satisfaction. A smooth and intuitive purchase process encourages players to spend money and reduces the risk of frustration or abandonment.

The first step in creating a seamless purchase experience is to streamline the purchase process. Players should be able to complete transactions with as few steps as possible. This includes minimizing the number of screens, reducing loading times, and providing clear and simple instructions.

Clear and intuitive navigation is essential. Players should be able to easily find the in-game store, browse items, and access their shopping cart. The layout should be logical and easy to understand, with clear labels and visual cues to guide players through the process.

Providing multiple payment options can enhance the purchase experience. Players have different preferences and access to payment methods, so offering a variety of options, such as credit cards, digital wallets, and mobile payments, can increase the likelihood of successful transactions.

Security is a major concern for players when making purchases. Developers should ensure that all transactions are secure and that player data is protected. This includes using secure payment gateways, encrypting sensitive information, and displaying security badges or messages to reassure players.

Feedback and confirmation are important in creating a seamless purchase experience. Players should receive immediate confirmation when they make a purchase, including visual and audio cues, confirmation messages, and receipts. This feedback helps reassure players that their transaction was successful and provides a sense of accomplishment.

Reducing friction in the payment process can prevent drop-offs and enhance the overall experience. This includes optimizing loading times, minimizing the number of required fields, and allowing players to save their payment information for future purchases. Reducing friction helps create a smoother and more enjoyable experience.

Personalization can enhance the purchase experience by providing relevant and tailored offers to individual players. Personalized recommendations, special discounts, and targeted messages can increase the likelihood of engagement and spending. Personalization helps create a more relevant and engaging experience for players.

Transparency is key to building trust with players. Players should always know what they are getting when they spend money and how much it will cost. Clear and honest communication about prices, offers, and rewards is essential. Hidden fees, ambiguous offers, and unclear terms can lead to frustration and distrust.

Ethical considerations should guide the design of the purchase experience. Developers should avoid using manipulative tactics that exploit players or create undue pressure to spend money. Fairness, transparency, and respect for the player's experience should be the guiding principles in designing the purchase process.

Testing and iteration are essential in refining the purchase experience. Developers should continuously gather data and feedback on how players interact with the purchase process and make adjustments based on this information. A/B testing can be used to experiment with different designs and determine which ones are most effective.

In summary, ensuring a seamless purchase experience involves streamlining the process, providing clear navigation, offering multiple payment options, ensuring security, providing feedback and confirmation, reducing friction, personalizing offers, maintaining transparency, and adhering to ethical considerations. By focusing on these principles, developers can create a more engaging and profitable purchase experience for players.

8.4 Feedback and Adaptation from User Data

Feedback and adaptation from user data are critical components of effective monetisation strategies. By continuously gathering and analyzing data on player behavior, developers can make informed decisions and refine their monetisation features to better meet player needs and preferences.

The first step in this process is to collect data on how players interact with the game and its monetisation features. This can include metrics such as playtime, in-game purchases, engagement with special offers, and feedback from surveys or in-game feedback tools. Data collection should be comprehensive and cover a wide range of player behaviors.

Once data is collected, it can be analyzed to identify patterns and trends. For example, developers might look for correlations between certain player behaviors and spending patterns. This analysis can provide insights into what drives player engagement and spending, and help identify areas for improvement.

A/B testing is a valuable tool for testing different monetisation strategies and features. By creating two or more versions of a feature and comparing their performance, developers can determine which approach is most effective. This method can be used to test different pricing strategies, reward structures, or user interface designs.

Player feedback is essential in refining monetisation features. Developers should actively seek feedback from players through surveys, focus groups, and in-game feedback tools.

This feedback can provide valuable insights into what players like and dislike about the monetisation mechanics and what improvements they would like to see.

Adaptation is the process of making changes based on data and feedback. This might involve adjusting prices, changing the frequency of special offers, or redesigning the user interface. The goal is to create a more engaging and satisfying experience for players while maximizing revenue.

Transparency with players is important when making changes based on feedback. Players should be informed about changes and the reasons behind them. This transparency helps build trust and reduces the risk of backlash from the player community.

Continuous learning is key to successful adaptation. The gaming industry is dynamic, with player preferences and market trends constantly evolving. Developers should stay informed about industry best practices, emerging technologies, and new monetisation models to keep their games competitive.

Ethical considerations should guide the use of data and feedback in monetisation. Developers should avoid exploiting players or using manipulative tactics to drive spending. Fairness and respect for the player's experience should be the guiding principles in designing monetisation strategies.

In summary, feedback and adaptation from user data are essential for creating effective and satisfying monetisation features. By continuously gathering data, analyzing patterns, seeking player feedback, and making informed changes, developers can create a more engaging and profitable gaming experience.

8.5 Avoiding Common UX Pitfalls in Monetisation

Avoiding common UX pitfalls in monetisation is crucial for maintaining player satisfaction and maximizing revenue. Poorly designed monetisation features can frustrate players and lead to decreased engagement and spending.

One common pitfall is creating a cluttered or confusing user interface. Players should be able to easily navigate the in-game store, browse items, and complete transactions. Clear and intuitive design, with logical layout and consistent visual cues, is essential for a smooth experience.

Another pitfall is using aggressive or intrusive monetisation tactics. Players should never feel pressured or manipulated into spending money. Pop-ups, forced ads, and constant reminders can disrupt the gameplay experience and lead to frustration. Monetisation features should be integrated seamlessly into the game and enhance rather than interrupt the player experience.

Lack of transparency is a major issue that can erode player trust. Players should always know what they are getting when they spend money and how much it will cost. Hidden fees, ambiguous offers, and unclear terms can lead to dissatisfaction and distrust. Clear and honest communication about prices, offers, and rewards is essential.

Complex or lengthy purchase processes can lead to abandonment. Players should be able to complete transactions quickly and easily, without unnecessary steps or delays. Optimizing loading times, minimizing the number of required fields, and providing multiple payment options can help reduce friction and enhance the purchase experience.

Neglecting player feedback is a significant pitfall. Developers should actively seek and respond to player feedback on monetisation features. Ignoring player concerns or failing to make necessary adjustments can lead to decreased satisfaction and engagement. Regularly gathering and analyzing feedback helps ensure that monetisation strategies are meeting player needs and preferences.

Failure to balance the in-game economy can also be problematic. In-game currency and items should be earnable through regular gameplay, but purchasing additional currency should provide a meaningful advantage. If the game feels pay-to-win or progress is too slow without spending money, players may become frustrated and disengage.

Ethical considerations are crucial in avoiding common UX pitfalls. Developers should avoid exploiting players or using manipulative tactics to drive spending. Fairness, transparency, and respect for the player's experience should guide all design decisions.

Testing and iteration are essential for avoiding UX pitfalls. Developers should continuously test different monetisation features and gather data on player interactions. A/B testing can provide valuable insights into what works and what doesn't, allowing for informed adjustments.

In summary, avoiding common UX pitfalls in monetisation involves creating a clear and intuitive user interface, avoiding aggressive tactics, maintaining transparency, streamlining the purchase process, responding to player feedback, balancing the in-game economy, adhering to ethical principles, and continuously testing and iterating. By focusing on these principles, developers can create a more satisfying and profitable gaming experience for players.

Chapter 9: Data Analytics and Monetisation

9.1 Role of Data in Monetisation

Data analytics plays a crucial role in the monetisation of mobile games. The ability to collect, analyze, and act on data allows developers to make informed decisions that can significantly impact revenue. This section explores the various ways in which data can be utilized to optimize monetisation strategies.

The first step in leveraging data for monetisation is the collection of relevant metrics. These metrics can include user acquisition costs, lifetime value (LTV) of players, retention rates, and in-game spending patterns. By understanding these metrics, developers can identify which aspects of their game are most profitable and which areas need improvement.

One key aspect of data-driven monetisation is segmentation. By dividing players into different segments based on their behavior, preferences, and spending habits, developers can tailor their monetisation strategies to each group. For example, high-spending players might be targeted with exclusive offers, while new players could be offered introductory discounts to encourage spending.

Predictive analytics is another powerful tool in monetisation. By analyzing historical data, developers can predict future spending patterns and behavior. This allows for proactive adjustments to monetisation strategies, such as offering time-limited discounts or introducing new in-game items that are likely to appeal to specific player segments.

A/B testing is a common practice in data-driven monetisation. By testing different monetisation strategies on small subsets of players, developers can determine which approach yields the best results. This iterative process ensures that the most effective strategies are implemented on a larger scale.

Data analytics also enables personalized experiences, which can enhance player engagement and spending. By understanding individual player preferences, developers can offer personalized recommendations for in-game purchases or suggest relevant content, increasing the likelihood of transactions.

Real-time analytics is essential for dynamic monetisation strategies. By monitoring player behavior in real-time, developers can respond quickly to changes and optimize their strategies on the fly. For example, if a particular in-game event is driving high engagement, developers can introduce special offers to capitalize on the increased activity.

The integration of machine learning algorithms can further enhance data-driven monetisation. These algorithms can identify complex patterns in player behavior that might not be apparent through traditional analysis. This deeper understanding can lead to more effective monetisation strategies and improved player experiences.

Data privacy and security are critical considerations in monetisation. Developers must ensure that player data is collected and stored securely, and that they comply with relevant data protection regulations. Transparency with players about data usage can also build trust and encourage engagement.

Effective data visualization is important for communicating insights and driving decision-making. Dashboards and reports that present key metrics and trends in an accessible format can help stakeholders understand the impact of monetisation strategies and identify areas for improvement.

In summary, data analytics is a cornerstone of successful monetisation in mobile games. By leveraging data to understand player behavior, optimize strategies, and personalize experiences, developers can maximize revenue while maintaining a positive player experience.

9.2 Key Metrics for Monetisation Analysis

Understanding and tracking key metrics is essential for effective monetisation analysis. These metrics provide insights into player behavior, spending patterns, and overall game performance. This section outlines some of the most important metrics for monetisation analysis and their relevance.

1. Daily Active Users (DAU) and Monthly Active Users (MAU): DAU and MAU are fundamental metrics that indicate the number of unique players engaging with the game on a daily and monthly basis. High DAU and MAU figures suggest a healthy, active player base, which is crucial for sustained monetisation.

2. Average Revenue Per User (ARPU): ARPU measures the average revenue generated per player over a specific period. It helps developers understand how much revenue each player contributes and can highlight the effectiveness of monetisation strategies.

3. Lifetime Value (LTV): LTV estimates the total revenue a player will generate throughout their engagement with the game. This metric is vital for determining the long-term profitability of players and guiding marketing and retention strategies.

4. Retention Rate: Retention rate measures the percentage of players who return to the game after their first session. High retention rates indicate that players find the game engaging and are more likely to make in-game purchases.

5. Churn Rate: Churn rate is the opposite of retention rate and indicates the percentage of players who stop playing the game. Understanding churn reasons can help developers address issues and improve retention.

6. Conversion Rate: Conversion rate measures the percentage of players who make an in-game purchase. A higher conversion rate suggests that monetisation strategies are effective in encouraging spending.

7. Average Transaction Value (ATV): ATV indicates the average amount spent by players per transaction. Monitoring ATV helps developers understand spending habits and optimize pricing strategies for virtual goods.

8. User Acquisition Cost (UAC): UAC measures the cost of acquiring a new player through marketing and advertising efforts. It is crucial for evaluating the efficiency of user acquisition campaigns and ensuring they are cost-effective.

9. Return on Investment (ROI): ROI calculates the profitability of marketing and monetisation efforts. A positive ROI indicates that the revenue generated exceeds the costs incurred, making the strategy viable.

10. Engagement Metrics: Metrics such as session length, frequency of play, and in-game interactions provide insights into player engagement. Higher engagement often correlates with increased spending and retention.

11. Ad Revenue Metrics: For games that incorporate advertising, metrics such as ad impressions, click-through rates (CTR), and effective cost per thousand impressions (eCPM) are crucial for assessing ad performance and revenue.

12. Player Segmentation Metrics: Segmenting players based on behavior, spending, and demographics allows for targeted monetisation strategies. Metrics related to different segments help identify the most valuable player groups.

13. Event Participation Metrics: Tracking participation in in-game events, challenges, and promotions provides insights into player interests and engagement levels. Successful events can drive significant revenue through increased activity and purchases.

14. Social Metrics: Metrics related to social interactions, such as friend referrals, social media shares, and in-game chat activity, can indicate community engagement and the effectiveness of social features in driving monetisation.

15. Feedback and Satisfaction Metrics: Player feedback, ratings, and satisfaction scores provide qualitative insights into player sentiment. Positive feedback can validate monetisation strategies, while negative feedback highlights areas for improvement.

By regularly monitoring these metrics, developers can gain a comprehensive understanding of their game's performance and make data-driven decisions to enhance monetisation. The interplay of these metrics offers a holistic view of player behavior and the impact of different strategies, enabling continuous optimization and growth.

9.3 Tools and Technologies for Data Analytics

The effective use of data analytics in mobile game monetisation relies on a suite of tools and technologies designed to collect, analyze, and interpret vast amounts of player data. This section explores some of the most commonly used tools and technologies in the industry.

1. Analytics Platforms: Platforms like Google Analytics, Firebase Analytics, and Flurry provide comprehensive tools for tracking player behavior, engagement, and monetisation metrics. These platforms offer dashboards, reporting capabilities, and real-time data insights, making it easier for developers to monitor key performance indicators (KPIs).

2. Business Intelligence (BI) Tools: BI tools such as Tableau, Power BI, and Looker enable developers to visualize data and create interactive dashboards. These tools help in identifying trends, patterns, and correlations within the data, facilitating informed decision-making.

3. Customer Relationship Management (CRM) Systems: CRM systems like Salesforce and HubSpot are essential for managing player interactions and segmenting players based on behavior and preferences. CRM data can be integrated with analytics platforms to provide a holistic view of player engagement and monetisation.

4. Machine Learning and AI Tools: Machine learning libraries and frameworks like TensorFlow, PyTorch, and Scikit-learn are used to build predictive models and algorithms that can forecast player behavior and optimize monetisation strategies. AI-driven insights help in personalizing player experiences and predicting future trends.

5. Data Warehousing Solutions: Data warehousing solutions like Amazon Redshift, Google BigQuery, and Snowflake allow for the storage and management of large volumes of player data. These solutions provide scalable and efficient ways to handle data from multiple sources, ensuring that it is accessible for analysis.

6. In-App Analytics SDKs: Software Development Kits (SDKs) such as Unity Analytics and GameAnalytics are specifically designed for in-app data collection. These SDKs can track player interactions, in-game purchases, and other critical metrics, providing developers with detailed insights into player behavior.

7. A/B Testing Tools: Tools like Optimizely, Split, and VWO facilitate A/B testing of different monetisation strategies. By testing variations of in-game offers, pricing, and features, developers can identify the most effective approaches and implement them broadly.

8. Ad Monetisation Platforms: Ad monetisation platforms like AdMob, Unity Ads, and IronSource provide tools for managing in-game advertising. These platforms offer analytics on ad performance, revenue generation, and player engagement with ads.

9. Data Integration Tools: Tools like Zapier, Fivetran, and Stitch help in integrating data from various sources into a unified platform. This integration ensures that all relevant data is available for analysis, enabling a comprehensive understanding of player behavior and monetisation.

10. Heatmap and Session Recording Tools: Tools like Hotjar and Crazy Egg provide heatmaps and session recordings that show how players interact with the game interface. These insights can help in optimizing user experience and identifying potential monetisation opportunities.

11. Feedback and Survey Tools: Platforms like SurveyMonkey and Typeform allow developers to collect player feedback and conduct surveys. Analyzing this qualitative data alongside quantitative metrics can provide a deeper understanding of player preferences and sentiment.

12. Retention and Engagement Tools: Tools like Leanplum, Braze, and Clevertap offer solutions for improving player retention and engagement through personalized messaging, push notifications, and in-app campaigns. These tools help in maintaining player interest and driving monetisation.

13. Cloud Computing Services: Cloud platforms like AWS, Google Cloud, and Azure provide the infrastructure needed to store, process, and analyze large datasets. These services offer scalability and flexibility, making it easier to handle the dynamic nature of player data.

14. Data Privacy and Security Tools: Ensuring data privacy and security is crucial in monetisation. Tools like DataGrail and OneTrust help in managing data compliance, protecting player information, and adhering to regulations such as GDPR and CCPA.

15. Custom Analytics Solutions: In some cases, developers may opt for custom-built analytics solutions tailored to their specific needs. These solutions can be developed using programming languages like Python and R, along with data processing frameworks like Apache Spark.

By leveraging these tools and technologies, developers can harness the power of data analytics to enhance their monetisation strategies. The integration of various tools allows for a comprehensive approach to data analysis, leading to more informed decisions and optimized revenue generation.

9.4 Interpreting and Acting on Data Insights

The process of interpreting and acting on data insights is critical for optimizing monetisation strategies in mobile games. This section outlines the steps involved in analyzing data, deriving actionable insights, and implementing changes to enhance revenue.

Step 1: Data Collection and Cleaning The first step in interpreting data is ensuring its accuracy and completeness. Data should be collected from reliable sources, and any inconsistencies or errors should be addressed. This may involve cleaning the data, removing duplicates, and filling in missing values.

Step 2: Data Analysis Once the data is clean, various analytical techniques can be applied to uncover patterns and trends. Descriptive analytics helps in summarizing the data and understanding the current state of monetisation. Tools like pivot tables, charts, and graphs can be used to visualize key metrics.

Step 3: Identifying Key Insights The next step is to identify key insights that can inform monetisation strategies. This involves looking for correlations and patterns within the data. For example, analyzing the relationship between player retention and in-game purchases can reveal which features or events drive spending.

Step 4: Hypothesis Testing To validate insights, hypothesis testing can be conducted. This involves making predictions based on the data and testing them through experiments. For example, if data suggests that players are more likely to make purchases during special events, a hypothesis can be tested by running similar events and measuring the results.

Step 5: Segmentation Analysis Segmenting players based on their behavior and preferences allows for targeted monetisation strategies. Segmentation analysis helps in understanding the unique needs of different player groups and tailoring offers accordingly. For instance, high-spending players might receive exclusive discounts, while new players could be offered introductory deals.

Step 6: Predictive Analytics Predictive analytics involves using historical data to forecast future trends. Machine learning models can predict player churn, spending patterns, and engagement levels. These predictions enable proactive measures, such as offering incentives to players at risk of churning.

Step 7: Personalization Personalizing the player experience can significantly impact monetisation. By using data to understand individual player preferences, developers can offer tailored recommendations for in-game purchases. Personalized offers and content can increase the likelihood of transactions and enhance player satisfaction.

Step 8: A/B Testing and Experimentation A/B testing is a method of comparing two versions of a feature or strategy to determine which performs better. By running experiments on small subsets of players, developers can test different monetisation approaches and select the most effective one. This iterative process ensures continuous improvement.

Step 9: Real-time Analytics Real-time analytics allows developers to monitor player behavior as it happens. This enables immediate adjustments to monetisation strategies based on current trends. For example, if a particular in-game event is driving high engagement, developers can introduce related offers to maximize revenue.

Step 10: Feedback Loop Establishing a feedback loop ensures that data insights continuously inform decision-making. This involves regularly reviewing performance metrics, analyzing the impact of implemented changes, and making necessary adjustments. Player feedback should also be incorporated to align strategies with player expectations.

Step 11: Collaboration and Communication Effective interpretation of data insights requires collaboration between different teams, including game designers, data analysts, and marketing specialists. Clear communication of insights and strategies ensures that everyone is aligned and working towards common goals.

Step 12: Ethical Considerations While interpreting and acting on data insights, it is important to consider ethical implications. Developers should ensure that monetisation strategies do not exploit players or encourage harmful behavior. Transparency with players about data usage and respecting their privacy is essential.

Step 13: Monitoring and Reporting Regular monitoring of key metrics and reporting on performance is crucial for ongoing optimization. Dashboards and reports that highlight trends, successes, and areas for improvement help in making data-driven decisions. Automated reporting tools can streamline this process and provide timely insights.

Step 14: Continuous Improvement The process of interpreting and acting on data insights should be continuous. As player behavior and market trends evolve, monetisation strategies should be regularly reviewed and updated. Continuous improvement ensures that the game remains competitive and profitable.

In conclusion, interpreting and acting on data insights involves a systematic approach to analyzing data, deriving actionable insights, and implementing changes. By following these steps, developers can optimize their monetisation strategies, enhance player experiences, and maximize revenue.

9.5 Case Studies of Data-Driven Monetisation Strategies

Case studies provide valuable insights into how data-driven monetisation strategies can be successfully implemented in mobile games. This section presents several case studies that highlight the effectiveness of data analytics in optimizing monetisation.

Case Study 1: Clash of Clans "Clash of Clans," developed by Supercell, is a prime example of a game that leverages data analytics for monetisation. The game uses A/B testing extensively to optimize in-game purchases and offers. By analyzing player behavior and spending patterns, Supercell identifies the most effective pricing strategies and promotions. For instance, limited-time offers and special events are tested on small player segments before being rolled out globally. This data-driven approach has contributed to the game's sustained revenue growth.

Case Study 2: Candy Crush Saga King's "Candy Crush Saga" employs predictive analytics to enhance player retention and spending. By analyzing historical data, the game predicts which players are at risk of churning and offers them targeted incentives to keep them engaged. Additionally, data insights are used to design levels and challenges that encourage in-game purchases. Personalized recommendations and dynamic pricing further enhance the monetisation strategy. As a result, "Candy Crush Saga" has maintained a loyal player base and generated significant revenue.

Case Study 3: Pokémon GO Niantic's "Pokémon GO" integrates real-time analytics to optimize in-game events and promotions. By monitoring player activity and engagement in real-time, the game adjusts its monetisation strategies on the fly. For example, during special events like Community Days, the game introduces exclusive offers and bundles based on real-time player behavior. This dynamic approach ensures that monetisation opportunities are maximized during peak engagement periods. The use of real-time data analytics has been instrumental in the game's success.

Case Study 4: Fortnite Epic Games' "Fortnite" utilizes machine learning to personalize the player experience and drive monetisation. The game collects vast amounts of player data to understand preferences and behavior. Machine learning algorithms analyze this data to recommend in-game purchases, such as skins and emotes, tailored to individual players. Additionally, A/B testing is used to refine monetisation strategies, ensuring that offers are appealing and effective. This data-driven personalization has contributed to "Fortnite's" massive revenue generation.

Case Study 5: Gardenscapes Playrix's "Gardenscapes" employs segmentation analysis to target different player groups with tailored monetisation strategies. By segmenting players based on their spending habits and engagement levels, the game offers personalized deals and discounts. For example, high-spending players receive exclusive offers, while new players are presented with introductory bundles. This targeted approach increases the likelihood of purchases and enhances player satisfaction. The use of data analytics has been key to the game's monetisation success.

Case Study 6: Angry Birds 2 Rovio's "Angry Birds 2" uses retention and engagement metrics to optimize its monetisation strategy. The game tracks player retention rates and session lengths to identify patterns and trends. Based on these insights, Rovio introduces features and events that enhance engagement and encourage spending. For instance, limited-time challenges and rewards are designed to keep players coming back and making in-game purchases. Data-driven decisions have helped "Angry Birds 2" maintain a strong player base and revenue stream.

Case Study 7: PUBG Mobile Tencent's "PUBG Mobile" leverages data integration tools to consolidate data from various sources and gain a comprehensive understanding of player behavior. The game uses this integrated data to personalize in-game offers and optimize ad placements. By analyzing ad performance metrics and player interactions, Tencent maximizes ad revenue without disrupting gameplay. The use of data analytics has been instrumental in balancing monetisation with player experience, contributing to the game's success.

Case Study 8: Homescapes Similar to "Gardenscapes," Playrix's "Homescapes" employs A/B testing and segmentation analysis to refine its monetisation strategies. The game tests different pricing models, offers, and events on small player segments to determine the most effective approaches. Insights from these tests are used to implement strategies that drive revenue and enhance player engagement. The continuous iteration and optimization based on data analytics have been key to "Homescapes'" monetisation success.

Case Study 9: Roblox "Roblox" incorporates extensive data analytics to understand player preferences and optimize its virtual economy. The platform tracks metrics related to user-generated content, player interactions, and in-game purchases. By analyzing this data, "Roblox" offers personalized recommendations and dynamic pricing for virtual items. Additionally, the platform uses machine learning to predict player spending patterns and adjust monetisation strategies accordingly. This data-driven approach has contributed to "Roblox's" substantial revenue growth.

Case Study 10: Clash Royale Supercell's "Clash Royale" uses predictive analytics and A/B testing to enhance its monetisation strategy. The game predicts which players are likely to make purchases and offers them targeted incentives. A/B testing is used to refine these offers and ensure their effectiveness. Additionally, data insights are used to design in-game events and challenges that drive engagement and spending. The integration of data analytics has been crucial to "Clash Royale's" monetisation success.

In conclusion, these case studies demonstrate the effectiveness of data-driven monetisation strategies in mobile games. By leveraging data analytics to understand player behavior, personalize experiences, and optimize offers, developers can significantly enhance revenue and maintain a positive player experience.

Chapter 10: Legal and Regulatory Considerations

10.1 Legal Framework for Mobile Game Monetisation

The legal framework for mobile game monetisation encompasses a range of laws and regulations that developers must adhere to in order to ensure compliance and protect player rights. This section provides an overview of key legal considerations and frameworks that impact the monetisation of mobile games.

1. Consumer Protection Laws: Consumer protection laws are designed to safeguard the rights of consumers and ensure fair practices. In the context of mobile game monetisation, these laws regulate issues such as transparency in pricing, advertising practices, and the protection of minors. Developers must ensure that in-game purchases and advertisements comply with these laws to avoid legal repercussions.

2. Data Protection Regulations: Data protection regulations, such as the General Data Protection Regulation (GDPR) in the European Union and the California Consumer Privacy Act (CCPA) in the United States, impose strict requirements on the collection, storage, and processing of personal data. Developers must obtain explicit consent from players before collecting their data and must implement measures to protect this data from unauthorized access or breaches.

3. Age Verification and Parental Consent: Many jurisdictions have specific regulations regarding the protection of minors in digital environments. Developers must implement age verification mechanisms to prevent underage players from accessing certain features or making in-game purchases without parental consent. Failure to comply with these regulations can result in significant fines and legal action.

4. In-App Purchase Regulations: In-app purchases are a common monetisation method in mobile games, but they are subject to various regulations. For example, the Federal Trade Commission (FTC) in the United States requires developers to clearly disclose the nature and cost of in-app purchases. Developers must also provide mechanisms for players to review and confirm their purchases to prevent unauthorized transactions.

5. Advertising Standards: Mobile games often include advertisements, which must comply with advertising standards and regulations. These standards ensure that ads are not misleading, offensive, or harmful. Developers must also provide players with options to opt-out of targeted advertising and ensure that ad content is appropriate for the game's audience.

6. Gambling and Loot Box Regulations: Some mobile games feature loot boxes or similar mechanisms that resemble gambling. Various jurisdictions have enacted regulations to address concerns about the addictive nature of these features and their impact on minors.

Developers must ensure that loot boxes are transparent, provide clear odds of winning, and avoid deceptive practices.

7. Intellectual Property Rights: Intellectual property rights (IPR) are critical in the gaming industry. Developers must ensure that their games do not infringe on the copyrights, trademarks, or patents of others. Additionally, they must protect their own intellectual property by registering trademarks and copyrights and enforcing these rights against unauthorized use.

8. Compliance with Platform Policies: Mobile games are typically distributed through app stores such as Google Play and Apple's App Store. These platforms have their own policies and guidelines regarding monetisation, data privacy, and content standards. Developers must comply with these policies to avoid removal from the platform and potential legal issues.

9. International Legal Considerations: Mobile games often have a global audience, which means developers must navigate a complex landscape of international laws and regulations. This includes complying with different consumer protection laws, data privacy regulations, and advertising standards in various countries. Localization of legal compliance is crucial for successful international monetisation.

10. Anti-Money Laundering (AML) Regulations: In-game currencies and virtual goods can potentially be used for money laundering activities. Developers must implement measures to detect and prevent money laundering, such as verifying player identities, monitoring transactions, and reporting suspicious activities to relevant authorities.

11. Terms of Service and End-User License Agreements (EULAs): Developers must create clear and comprehensive terms of service and EULAs that outline the rights and responsibilities of players. These agreements should cover issues such as in-game purchases, data privacy, user conduct, and dispute resolution. Players must agree to these terms before accessing the game.

12. Regulatory Compliance Monitoring: Ongoing monitoring of regulatory changes and compliance requirements is essential. The legal landscape for mobile game monetisation is constantly evolving, and developers must stay informed about new laws and regulations that may impact their games. Regular audits and legal reviews can help ensure continued compliance.

13. Penalties for Non-Compliance: Failure to comply with legal and regulatory requirements can result in severe penalties, including fines, legal action, and reputational damage. Developers must take compliance seriously and implement robust measures to avoid potential legal issues.

14. Best Practices for Legal Compliance: To ensure legal compliance, developers should adopt best practices such as conducting regular legal audits, providing training for staff on legal requirements, and working with legal experts to navigate complex regulations. Clear documentation and transparent communication with players are also essential.

15. Ethical Considerations: Beyond legal compliance, developers should consider the ethical implications of their monetisation strategies. Ensuring that monetisation practices are fair, transparent, and respectful of player rights can help build trust and loyalty among players.

In conclusion, the legal framework for mobile game monetisation encompasses a wide range of regulations and requirements. Developers must navigate these complexities to ensure compliance, protect player rights, and avoid legal issues. By adopting best practices and staying informed about regulatory changes, developers can create a sustainable and legally compliant monetisation strategy.

10.2 Regulatory Issues in Different Regions

Regulatory issues related to mobile game monetisation vary significantly across different regions. Understanding these regional differences is crucial for developers aiming to launch and monetize their games globally. This section explores key regulatory issues in major markets around the world.

1. North America: In North America, particularly the United States and Canada, regulatory frameworks focus heavily on data privacy, consumer protection, and advertising standards. The Federal Trade Commission (FTC) in the U.S. enforces regulations related to in-app purchases, advertising, and data privacy. The Children's Online Privacy Protection Act (COPPA) requires parental consent for collecting data from children under 13. In Canada, the Personal Information Protection and Electronic Documents Act (PIPEDA) governs data privacy.

2. European Union: The European Union has some of the strictest data protection regulations globally, primarily governed by the General Data Protection Regulation (GDPR). GDPR mandates stringent data privacy measures, including explicit consent for data collection and the right to be forgotten. The EU also focuses on consumer protection and has introduced regulations for transparent loot box mechanics to address concerns about gambling-like features in games.

3. Asia: Asia is a diverse market with varying regulatory landscapes. In China, the government enforces strict regulations on online gaming, including real-name verification, time limits for minors, and content censorship. The Cyberspace Administration of China (CAC) regulates data privacy and cybersecurity. In Japan, the Payment Services Act governs in-game purchases and virtual currencies, while the Consumer Affairs Agency monitors consumer protection.

4. South Korea: South Korea has a robust regulatory framework for online games, including regulations on game addiction, data privacy, and consumer protection. The Game Rating and Administration Committee (GRAC) oversees game content ratings, and the Korea Communications Commission (KCC) regulates data privacy. Developers must also comply with the Act on the Promotion of Information and Communications Network Utilization and Information Protection.

5. Australia: In Australia, the Australian Competition and Consumer Commission (ACCC) enforces consumer protection laws, including transparency in in-app purchases and advertising. The Office of the Australian Information Commissioner (OAIC) oversees data privacy regulations under the Privacy Act. Developers must ensure that their games comply with these regulations to avoid penalties.

6. Latin America: Latin American countries, including Brazil and Mexico, have emerging regulatory frameworks for mobile games. Brazil's General Data Protection Law (LGPD) is similar to the GDPR, focusing on data privacy and protection. Consumer protection agencies in these countries monitor in-app purchases and advertising practices to ensure fairness and transparency.

7. Middle East: Regulatory frameworks in the Middle East vary, with some countries adopting stringent controls on online content and data privacy. For example, the United Arab Emirates (UAE) has regulations governing online gaming content and data protection. Developers must navigate cultural sensitivities and comply with local laws to operate successfully in this region.

8. Russia: Russia has implemented strict data localization laws, requiring developers to store personal data of Russian citizens on servers located within the country. The Federal Service for Supervision of Communications, Information Technology, and Mass Media (Roskomnadzor) enforces these regulations. Developers must also comply with laws related to online content and consumer protection.

9. India: India's regulatory landscape for mobile games is evolving, with increasing focus on data privacy and consumer protection. The Personal Data Protection Bill (PDPB) aims to regulate data privacy, while the Ministry of Electronics and Information Technology (MeitY) oversees digital content and cybersecurity. Developers should stay informed about regulatory changes in this rapidly growing market.

10. Africa: Africa's regulatory environment for mobile games is still developing, with varying levels of enforcement across different countries. South Africa has introduced the Protection of Personal Information Act (POPIA) to regulate data privacy. Developers targeting African markets should be aware of local consumer protection laws and emerging data privacy regulations.

11. Global Compliance Strategies: Given the diverse regulatory landscapes, developers must adopt strategies to ensure global compliance. This includes implementing robust data privacy measures, conducting regular legal audits, and working with local legal experts to navigate regional regulations. Additionally, clear communication with players about data usage and in-app purchases can build trust and ensure compliance.

12. Challenges and Opportunities: Navigating regional regulatory differences presents both challenges and opportunities. Compliance with stringent regulations can be resource-intensive, but it also opens doors to new markets and enhances player trust. Developers who prioritize compliance can differentiate themselves in the competitive mobile gaming industry.

13. Future Trends: As the mobile gaming industry continues to grow, regulatory frameworks are likely to evolve. Developers should stay informed about emerging trends, such as increased scrutiny of loot boxes, enhanced data privacy regulations, and new consumer protection laws. Proactive compliance can help developers stay ahead of regulatory changes and maintain a positive reputation.

14. Case Studies: Examining case studies of successful compliance strategies can provide valuable insights. For example, games like "Fortnite" and "Pokémon GO" have successfully navigated regulatory challenges in multiple regions by implementing comprehensive compliance measures and engaging with regulatory authorities.

15. Best Practices: Adopting best practices for regulatory compliance involves regular training for staff, continuous monitoring of regulatory changes, and maintaining transparent communication with players. Developers should also consider investing in compliance management tools to streamline the process and ensure adherence to global regulations.

In conclusion, understanding and navigating regulatory issues in different regions is essential for successful mobile game monetisation. By staying informed about regional regulations, adopting best practices, and proactively addressing compliance challenges, developers can ensure that their games meet legal requirements and build trust with players globally.

10.3 Protecting Player Privacy and Data

Protecting player privacy and data is a critical aspect of mobile game development and monetisation. Ensuring that player data is collected, stored, and used responsibly not only helps in complying with legal regulations but also builds trust with players. This section outlines key strategies and practices for protecting player privacy and data.

1. Data Minimization: Data minimization involves collecting only the data that is necessary for the game's functionality and monetisation. By limiting the amount of data collected, developers can reduce the risk of data breaches and ensure compliance with data protection regulations. This practice also aligns with the principles of privacy by design.

2. Transparent Data Collection: Transparency in data collection is essential for building trust with players. Developers should clearly communicate what data is being collected, how it will be used, and who it will be shared with. Privacy policies should be easily accessible and written in simple, understandable language.

3. Explicit Consent: Obtaining explicit consent from players before collecting their data is a fundamental requirement of many data protection regulations, such as GDPR. Developers should implement mechanisms for players to provide informed consent and offer options to withdraw consent at any time.

4. Secure Data Storage: Ensuring the secure storage of player data is crucial for protecting it from unauthorized access and breaches. Developers should use encryption and other security measures to protect data both in transit and at rest. Regular security audits and vulnerability assessments can help identify and address potential weaknesses.

5. Anonymization and Pseudonymization: Anonymizing or pseudonymizing player data can further enhance privacy protection. By removing or masking personal identifiers, developers can reduce the risk of data being linked back to individual players. These techniques can be particularly useful for data analytics and research purposes.

6. Access Controls: Implementing strict access controls ensures that only authorized personnel have access to player data. Role-based access control (RBAC) can help manage permissions and prevent unauthorized access. Regular reviews of access permissions are essential to maintaining security.

7. Data Breach Response Plan: Having a robust data breach response plan is essential for quickly addressing any data breaches that occur. This plan should include procedures for identifying and containing the breach, notifying affected players and regulatory authorities, and mitigating any damage. Regular drills and updates to the plan can ensure preparedness.

8. Third-Party Data Handling: When working with third-party vendors and partners, developers must ensure that these entities also comply with data protection standards. Contracts with third parties should include data protection clauses, and regular audits should be conducted to verify compliance.

9. Children's Privacy: Protecting the privacy of children is particularly important, as they are more vulnerable to exploitation. Developers should comply with regulations such as COPPA and GDPR-K, which impose additional requirements for data collection from minors. Age verification mechanisms and parental consent processes should be implemented.

10. User Rights: Data protection regulations grant players various rights regarding their data, such as the right to access, rectify, and delete their data. Developers should provide easy-to-use mechanisms for players to exercise these rights and respond promptly to their requests.

11. Privacy by Design: Integrating privacy by design principles into the game development process ensures that privacy considerations are addressed from the outset. This approach involves incorporating privacy features and safeguards into the design and architecture of the game.

12. Regular Training: Regular training for staff on data protection practices and regulatory requirements is essential. This training should cover topics such as secure data handling, recognizing phishing attempts, and responding to data breaches. Keeping staff informed and vigilant can help prevent data protection issues.

13. Continuous Monitoring: Continuous monitoring of data protection practices is necessary to ensure ongoing compliance. This includes regular audits, security assessments, and monitoring of data access and usage. Automated tools and solutions can assist in maintaining continuous oversight.

14. Privacy Impact Assessments (PIAs): Conducting Privacy Impact Assessments (PIAs) helps identify and mitigate privacy risks associated with new features or changes to the game. PIAs involve evaluating the potential impact on player privacy and implementing measures to address any identified risks.

15. Compliance with Global Regulations: As mobile games often have a global audience, developers must comply with data protection regulations in different regions. This includes understanding the specific requirements of laws such as GDPR, CCPA, and LGPD, and implementing measures to meet these requirements.

In conclusion, protecting player privacy and data is a multifaceted challenge that requires a comprehensive approach. By adopting best practices and implementing robust data protection measures, developers can ensure compliance with legal regulations, build trust with players, and create a safe and secure gaming environment.

10.4 Complying with Consumer Protection Laws

Complying with consumer protection laws is essential for mobile game developers to ensure fair practices, protect player rights, and avoid legal repercussions. This section outlines key aspects of consumer protection laws and strategies for compliance in the context of mobile game monetisation.

1. Transparency in In-App Purchases: Consumer protection laws require transparency in the pricing and nature of in-app purchases. Developers must clearly disclose the cost of in-app items, any recurring charges, and the terms of purchase. Players should be able to easily review and confirm their purchases before completing the transaction.

2. Advertising Standards: Advertisements within mobile games must comply with advertising standards to ensure they are not misleading, offensive, or harmful. Developers should avoid exaggerated claims about in-game items or benefits and ensure that ad content is appropriate for the game's audience. Providing options for players to opt-out of targeted advertising is also important.

3. Protection of Minors: Special considerations are required for protecting minors in mobile games. This includes implementing age verification mechanisms and obtaining parental consent for in-app purchases and data collection from children. Developers must comply with regulations such as COPPA and GDPR-K that specifically address the protection of children's privacy and rights.

4. Refund Policies: Consumer protection laws often mandate clear and fair refund policies for in-app purchases. Developers should provide mechanisms for players to request refunds and ensure that these policies are communicated transparently. Handling refund requests promptly and fairly can help maintain player trust and avoid disputes.

5. Avoiding Predatory Practices: Developers should avoid predatory monetisation practices that exploit players, such as excessively aggressive microtransactions or pay-to-win mechanics. Consumer protection laws and industry guidelines discourage practices that manipulate players into making unintended or excessive purchases.

6. Clear Terms of Service: Terms of service (ToS) and end-user license agreements (EULAs) should be clear, comprehensive, and easily accessible. These agreements should outline the rights and responsibilities of players, including terms related to in-app purchases, data privacy, and user conduct. Players must agree to these terms before accessing the game.

7. Disclosure of Loot Box Odds: In regions where loot boxes are regulated, developers must disclose the odds of winning specific items. This transparency helps players make informed decisions and addresses concerns about gambling-like features in games. Implementing clear and accessible disclosures can enhance compliance and player trust.

8. Handling Player Complaints: Developers should establish procedures for handling player complaints and disputes. Providing accessible channels for players to raise concerns and resolving issues promptly can prevent escalation to regulatory authorities. Documenting and reviewing complaints can also help identify areas for improvement in monetisation practices.

9. Monitoring Regulatory Changes: The regulatory landscape for consumer protection is constantly evolving. Developers must stay informed about changes in laws and regulations that impact their games. Regular legal audits and consultations with legal experts can help ensure ongoing compliance and adapt to new requirements.

10. Ethical Monetisation: Beyond legal compliance, adopting ethical monetisation practices can enhance player satisfaction and loyalty. This includes ensuring that monetisation strategies are fair, transparent, and respectful of player rights. Ethical considerations should guide the design and implementation of in-app purchases and advertising.

11. Compliance with Platform Policies: Mobile game platforms, such as Google Play and Apple's App Store, have their own policies and guidelines for consumer protection. Developers must comply with these platform policies to avoid removal from the app stores and potential legal issues. Regularly reviewing and adhering to platform guidelines is essential.

12. Educating Players: Educating players about their rights and the terms of in-app purchases can help prevent misunderstandings and disputes. Providing clear information and FAQs about in-app purchases, refund policies, and data privacy can empower players to make informed decisions.

13. Implementing User-Friendly Interfaces: User-friendly interfaces for in-app purchases and settings can enhance transparency and compliance. This includes clear labeling of purchase buttons, easy access to purchase history, and straightforward processes for requesting refunds or adjusting privacy settings.

14. Cross-Border Compliance: For games with a global audience, developers must navigate cross-border compliance challenges. This includes understanding and adhering to consumer protection laws in different regions. Localization of terms of service, privacy policies, and purchase disclosures can help ensure compliance in various markets.

15. Case Studies and Best Practices: Studying case studies of successful compliance strategies can provide valuable insights. Learning from industry best practices and avoiding common pitfalls can help developers implement effective consumer protection measures and enhance player trust.

In conclusion, complying with consumer protection laws is crucial for mobile game developers to ensure fair practices and protect player rights. By adopting transparent, ethical, and player-centric monetisation strategies, developers can enhance compliance, build trust, and create a positive gaming experience.

10.5 Navigating Legal Challenges in Monetisation

Navigating legal challenges in mobile game monetisation requires a thorough understanding of the regulatory landscape and proactive measures to ensure compliance. This section outlines key legal challenges and strategies for addressing them effectively.

1. Data Privacy Regulations: Data privacy regulations, such as GDPR and CCPA, impose stringent requirements on how player data is collected, stored, and processed. Developers must implement robust data protection measures, obtain explicit consent from players, and provide mechanisms for players to exercise their data rights. Regular audits and compliance checks are essential to avoid legal penalties.

2. Age Verification and Parental Consent: Ensuring compliance with age verification and parental consent requirements is crucial for protecting minors. Developers should implement reliable age verification mechanisms and obtain parental consent for data collection and in-app purchases involving children. Failure to comply with these regulations can result in significant fines and reputational damage.

3. In-App Purchase Transparency: Transparency in in-app purchases is a common legal requirement. Developers must clearly disclose the cost, nature, and terms of in-app purchases. Providing players with clear information and options to review and confirm purchases can prevent misunderstandings and legal disputes.

4. Advertising Compliance: Mobile games often include advertisements, which must comply with advertising standards and regulations. Developers should ensure that ads are not misleading, offensive, or inappropriate for the game's audience. Providing players with options to opt-out of targeted advertising and adhering to platform guidelines can enhance compliance.

5. Loot Box Regulations: Loot boxes and similar mechanics are subject to increasing regulatory scrutiny due to their resemblance to gambling. Developers must disclose the odds of winning specific items, implement measures to prevent excessive spending, and avoid deceptive practices. Compliance with regional regulations, such as those in the EU and China, is essential.

6. Intellectual Property Protection: Protecting intellectual property (IP) is critical for mobile game developers. This includes securing copyrights, trademarks, and patents for game content, and ensuring that the game does not infringe on the IP rights of others. Developers should also monitor and enforce their IP rights to prevent unauthorized use.

7. Consumer Protection Laws: Consumer protection laws mandate fair practices in in-app purchases, refunds, and advertising. Developers must provide clear terms of service, offer fair refund policies, and handle player complaints promptly. Compliance with these laws can prevent legal disputes and enhance player trust.

8. Cross-Border Legal Challenges: Mobile games often have a global audience, which means developers must navigate different legal requirements in various regions. This includes complying with data protection laws, consumer protection regulations, and advertising standards in different countries. Localization of legal compliance efforts is essential for global success.

9. Platform Policies: Compliance with platform policies, such as those of Google Play and Apple's App Store, is necessary for distribution. Developers must adhere to guidelines related to in-app purchases, data privacy, and content standards to avoid removal from these platforms and potential legal issues.

10. Anti-Money Laundering (AML) Measures: In-game currencies and virtual goods can be used for money laundering activities. Developers must implement AML measures, such as verifying player identities, monitoring transactions, and reporting suspicious activities. Compliance with AML regulations can prevent legal liabilities and protect the game's integrity.

11. Regulatory Changes: The regulatory landscape for mobile games is constantly evolving. Developers must stay informed about new laws and regulations that impact monetisation. Regular legal audits, consultations with legal experts, and proactive adaptation to regulatory changes are essential for ongoing compliance.

12. Ethical Considerations: Beyond legal compliance, developers should consider the ethical implications of their monetisation strategies. Ensuring that practices are fair, transparent, and respectful of player rights can enhance player trust and loyalty. Ethical considerations should guide the design and implementation of in-app purchases and advertising.

13. Case Studies and Best Practices: Examining case studies of successful compliance strategies can provide valuable insights. Learning from industry best practices and avoiding common pitfalls can help developers navigate legal challenges and enhance compliance.

14. Training and Education: Regular training and education for staff on legal requirements and best practices are essential. This includes training on data protection, consumer rights, and ethical monetisation. Keeping staff informed and vigilant can help prevent legal issues and ensure compliance.

15. Collaboration with Legal Experts: Collaborating with legal experts and consultants can provide valuable guidance on navigating complex legal challenges. Legal experts can help developers interpret regulations, implement compliance measures, and address potential legal issues proactively.

In conclusion, navigating legal challenges in mobile game monetisation requires a comprehensive approach to compliance. By staying informed about regulatory changes, adopting best practices, and proactively addressing legal requirements, developers can ensure compliance, protect player rights, and create a positive gaming experience.

Chapter 10: Legal and Regulatory Considerations

Chapter 11: Global Perspectives on Monetisation

11.1 Monetisation Trends in Different Markets

Monetisation trends in mobile games vary significantly across different global markets. Understanding these differences is crucial for developers aiming to maximize their revenue potential. In North America, the market is characterized by a high willingness to spend on in-app purchases (IAPs) and subscriptions. Players in this region often value premium content and are more likely to pay for game enhancements that improve their gaming experience.

In contrast, European markets exhibit diverse monetisation behaviors. Western European countries, such as the UK, Germany, and France, display similar tendencies to North America with a strong preference for IAPs and premium content. However, Southern and Eastern European countries often favor ad-supported models due to lower disposable incomes.

Asia represents a unique and highly lucrative market for mobile game developers. Countries like China, Japan, and South Korea have a deeply ingrained culture of mobile gaming, with players spending significantly on virtual goods and in-game currency. The success of the Free-to-Play (F2P) model in these regions can be attributed to the high engagement levels and the social nature of gaming communities.

In emerging markets such as India and Southeast Asia, monetisation strategies need to be tailored to lower-income populations. Ad-supported models and affordable microtransactions are more effective in these regions. Developers often experiment with local pricing strategies and culturally relevant content to enhance player engagement and spending.

Latin America presents a mixed landscape. While some countries like Brazil and Mexico have growing middle-class populations willing to spend on mobile games, others rely heavily on ad-supported models. Economic volatility in the region necessitates flexible and adaptive monetisation strategies.

Africa, although still developing in terms of mobile gaming, shows promise with increasing smartphone penetration. The primary monetisation strategy here revolves around ad-supported models, with gradual adoption of microtransactions as the market matures.

Understanding these regional differences allows developers to implement targeted monetisation strategies, enhancing their global revenue potential. Analyzing market-specific data and player behavior is essential for optimizing monetisation efforts.

11.2 Cultural Differences in Player Spending

Cultural factors play a significant role in influencing player spending behaviors in mobile games. In Asia, for instance, the concept of "face" or social standing can drive players to spend more on virtual goods to showcase their status within gaming communities. This phenomenon is particularly evident in China and South Korea, where players invest heavily in cosmetic items and rare in-game assets.

In Western cultures, individualism often shapes spending patterns. Players are more likely to spend on enhancing their personal gaming experience, such as purchasing premium content or unlocking additional features. The emphasis is on personal satisfaction and enjoyment rather than social recognition.

In Japan, the concept of "gacha" or loot boxes is deeply rooted in the gaming culture. Players are accustomed to spending on randomized rewards, and this model has proven to be highly profitable. However, this practice has faced criticism and regulatory scrutiny in Western markets, highlighting the need for cultural sensitivity in monetisation strategies.

In Latin America, social connectivity and community play a pivotal role in gaming. Players are more inclined to spend on features that enhance social interactions, such as multiplayer modes and community-driven events. Developers often focus on creating engaging social experiences to drive monetisation in this region.

Cultural attitudes towards gambling also impact spending behaviors. In regions where gambling is culturally accepted, such as Macau and Las Vegas, players are more comfortable with spending on chance-based mechanics like loot boxes. Conversely, in cultures with stricter views on gambling, developers need to adopt transparent and fair monetisation practices to gain player trust.

Localization of content is another crucial aspect of catering to cultural differences. Translating the game and adapting it to local customs, holidays, and events can significantly boost player engagement and spending. For example, incorporating local festivals and traditions into game events can resonate deeply with players, encouraging them to spend on related virtual items.

Ultimately, understanding and respecting cultural differences is key to successful monetisation in global markets. Developers must conduct thorough research and engage with local communities to tailor their strategies effectively.

11.3 Localisation of Monetisation Strategies

Localisation goes beyond mere translation; it involves adapting the entire gaming experience to resonate with the local audience. Successful localisation of monetisation strategies requires a deep understanding of regional preferences, cultural nuances, and economic conditions.

For instance, in Japan, integrating traditional and contemporary cultural elements into the game can significantly enhance player engagement. Developers often collaborate with local artists and designers to create culturally relevant content. Additionally, pricing strategies must reflect local purchasing power and economic conditions. Offering region-specific discounts and bundles can make in-app purchases more appealing to players.

In China, the "red envelope" tradition, where money is gifted during special occasions, has inspired in-game gifting systems. Developers have created virtual red envelopes that players can send to friends, incorporating a familiar cultural practice into the gaming experience. This not only enhances player engagement but also drives monetisation through social interactions.

In India, where price sensitivity is high, microtransactions at lower price points are more effective. Offering affordable in-game purchases and regional payment options, such as mobile wallets and UPI, can significantly increase conversion rates. Developers also leverage local festivals and events to introduce time-limited offers and exclusive content, encouraging players to spend.

Localising monetisation strategies also involves understanding regulatory landscapes. In regions with stringent regulations on in-game spending, such as Belgium and the Netherlands, developers must ensure compliance by removing or modifying loot box mechanics. Transparent and ethical monetisation practices build trust and foster long-term player loyalty.

Furthermore, regional preferences for specific game genres should inform monetisation strategies. For example, strategy games are highly popular in South Korea, where players are willing to spend on competitive advantages and exclusive content. In contrast, casual and hyper-casual games dominate the Indian market, requiring ad-supported models and frequent updates to retain player interest.

Effective localisation requires collaboration with local experts, continuous market research, and flexibility to adapt strategies based on player feedback. By tailoring monetisation approaches to regional preferences, developers can maximize their revenue potential while providing a satisfying and culturally relevant gaming experience.

11.4 Success Stories from Various Regions

Success stories from different regions provide valuable insights into effective monetisation strategies. In China, the game "Honor of Kings" by Tencent has achieved remarkable success by leveraging the social nature of Chinese gamers. The game incorporates popular cultural elements and offers a wide range of cosmetic items, driving significant revenue through in-app purchases. Regular updates and community events keep players engaged and spending.

In the United States, "Fortnite" by Epic Games has set a benchmark for monetisation through its innovative use of the Battle Pass system. By offering a tiered reward system that encourages continuous play and spending, "Fortnite" has maintained high player engagement and consistent revenue. The game's ability to adapt and introduce new content based on player preferences has been key to its success.

Japan's "Puzzle & Dragons" by GungHo Online Entertainment exemplifies the power of the gacha system. By combining puzzle gameplay with collectible monsters, the game has captivated players and generated substantial revenue through randomized rewards. The game's success highlights the importance of understanding and integrating local gaming preferences into monetisation strategies.

In India, "Ludo King" by Gametion Technologies has capitalized on the popularity of the traditional board game Ludo. By offering an ad-supported model with optional in-app purchases for premium features, the game has reached a wide audience and generated significant ad revenue. The game's offline multiplayer mode and culturally resonant themes have contributed to its widespread appeal.

South Korea's "Lineage M" by NCSoft has demonstrated the effectiveness of a subscription-based model in the MMORPG genre. The game's subscription service offers exclusive benefits and content, driving sustained revenue from dedicated players. The success of "Lineage M" underscores the potential of subscription models in regions with high engagement in specific game genres.

Brazil's "Free Fire" by Garena has achieved success through a combination of free-to-play and ad-supported models. The game's accessibility, frequent updates, and localized content have resonated with the Brazilian audience. In-game events and collaborations with local influencers have further boosted player engagement and spending.

These success stories illustrate the importance of tailoring monetisation strategies to regional preferences and market conditions. By understanding local player behaviors, cultural nuances, and economic factors, developers can create effective monetisation models that drive revenue and enhance player satisfaction.

11.5 Adapting to Global Market Changes

Adapting to global market changes is essential for sustaining long-term success in mobile game monetisation. The gaming industry is dynamic, with evolving player preferences, technological advancements, and regulatory shifts requiring continuous adaptation.

One significant trend is the increasing importance of player data and analytics. By leveraging data insights, developers can identify emerging trends, player behaviors, and market demands. For example, real-time analytics can reveal which in-game items are most popular in different regions, allowing developers to adjust pricing and promotional strategies accordingly.

Technological advancements, such as the rise of 5G and cloud gaming, are transforming the mobile gaming landscape. These technologies enable more complex and graphically intensive games, creating new monetisation opportunities. Developers can explore subscription-based models for premium gaming experiences and invest in cloud gaming platforms to reach a broader audience.

Regulatory changes also necessitate adaptation. For instance, data privacy regulations like the GDPR in Europe and CCPA in California require developers to implement robust data protection measures. Compliance with these regulations builds player trust and ensures the sustainability of monetisation strategies.

Economic factors, such as fluctuations in currency exchange rates and purchasing power, influence player spending behaviors. Developers must monitor global economic trends and adjust pricing strategies to maintain affordability and competitiveness in different markets.

The COVID-19 pandemic has accelerated digital adoption and increased mobile game usage. Developers who quickly adapted to this surge by introducing new content, virtual events, and flexible pricing models have seen substantial revenue growth. The pandemic has underscored the importance of agility and responsiveness in the face of unforeseen market changes.

Global collaborations and partnerships are becoming increasingly important. By partnering with local influencers, brands, and payment providers, developers can enhance their market presence and drive player engagement. For example, collaborations with popular regional influencers can amplify marketing efforts and reach new player segments.

Continuous learning and adaptation are key to navigating global market changes. Developers should stay informed about industry trends, participate in gaming conferences, and engage with player communities to gather feedback and insights. By remaining proactive and responsive, developers can ensure their monetisation strategies remain effective and relevant in an ever-changing global market.

Chapter 12: Monetisation in Emerging Technologies

12.1 Monetisation in AR and VR Games

Augmented Reality (AR) and Virtual Reality (VR) are transforming the gaming landscape, offering immersive experiences that open up new monetisation opportunities. AR and VR games create unique interactions by blending digital content with the real world or providing fully immersive virtual environments.

In AR games, in-app purchases often include virtual items that enhance real-world interactions. For example, players can purchase exclusive AR filters, avatars, and accessories. Location-based AR games, like "Pokémon GO," have successfully monetized through special events and limited-time offers tied to real-world locations. These strategies leverage the physical movement of players, encouraging exploration and spending.

VR games offer a different set of monetisation strategies. Given the immersive nature of VR, players are willing to invest in premium content that enhances their virtual experiences. This includes purchasing new game levels, environments, and interactive elements. Subscription models are also gaining traction in the VR space, providing players with continuous access to new content and features.

Advertising in AR and VR games presents unique challenges and opportunities. Non-intrusive, immersive ads that blend seamlessly with the game environment are more effective. For instance, virtual billboards in a VR racing game or branded items in an AR scavenger hunt can enhance player experience while generating revenue.

Monetising AR and VR games also involves leveraging hardware and peripheral sales. VR headsets, controllers, and AR glasses can be bundled with exclusive in-game content, driving both hardware and software sales. Partnerships with hardware manufacturers can lead to co-branded experiences that attract a dedicated player base.

Developers must also consider the technological limitations and high entry costs associated with AR and VR. Ensuring broad accessibility and affordability is key to expanding the player base. Offering a mix of free content and premium add-ons can attract a wider audience while providing monetisation opportunities for engaged players.

The future of AR and VR game monetisation will likely see advancements in user-generated content. Platforms that allow players to create and sell their own virtual items and experiences can foster a vibrant economy within the game. This not only drives engagement but also provides developers with a share of player-to-player transactions.

To maximize the potential of AR and VR monetisation, developers must stay abreast of technological advancements and continuously experiment with new strategies. By offering innovative and immersive experiences, AR and VR games can capture player interest and drive sustainable revenue growth.

12.2 Blockchain and Cryptocurrency in Gaming

Blockchain technology and cryptocurrency are poised to revolutionize monetisation in mobile games. By enabling decentralized, transparent, and secure transactions, blockchain offers new possibilities for in-game economies and player ownership.

One of the key applications of blockchain in gaming is the creation of non-fungible tokens (NFTs). NFTs represent unique digital assets that players can own, trade, and sell. In-game items, characters, and even entire virtual properties can be tokenized as NFTs, providing players with true ownership. This model encourages player investment and engagement, as players can profit from their virtual assets.

Cryptocurrency can also be integrated into game economies as a medium of exchange. Players can earn, spend, and trade cryptocurrencies within the game, creating a dynamic and real-world connected economy. For example, players might earn cryptocurrency rewards for completing challenges or participating in events, which they can then use to purchase in-game items or exchange for real money.

Blockchain-based games can also implement decentralized finance (DeFi) mechanisms, such as staking and yield farming. Players can stake their in-game assets or cryptocurrency to earn passive income, further enhancing their investment in the game. These mechanisms create a deeper level of engagement and financial incentive for players.

Transparency and security are significant advantages of blockchain in gaming. Blockchain ensures that all transactions and ownership records are immutable and publicly verifiable. This reduces fraud and enhances player trust in the game's economy. Smart contracts can automate and enforce rules, ensuring fair and transparent gameplay.

Developers can leverage Initial Coin Offerings (ICOs) and token sales to fund game development and expansion. By issuing their own cryptocurrency or tokens, developers can raise capital directly from their player base and investors. This approach aligns the interests of developers and players, as the success of the game directly impacts the value of the tokens.

However, integrating blockchain and cryptocurrency into games presents challenges. Regulatory uncertainty, especially regarding cryptocurrency, requires careful compliance and risk management. The volatility of cryptocurrency prices can also impact the stability of in-game economies. Developers must design mechanisms to mitigate these risks and ensure a balanced and sustainable economy.

Adopting blockchain and cryptocurrency in gaming requires a forward-thinking approach and continuous innovation. As the technology matures and regulatory frameworks evolve, these tools will offer unprecedented opportunities for game monetisation and player engagement.

12.3 The Future of Monetisation with AI

Artificial Intelligence (AI) is transforming the future of game monetisation by enabling personalized and adaptive experiences. AI-driven algorithms can analyze player behavior, preferences, and spending patterns to tailor monetisation strategies in real-time.

Personalized in-game offers are one of the most promising applications of AI. By analyzing player data, AI can predict what types of offers are most likely to convert each player. For example, a player who frequently purchases cosmetic items might receive personalized offers for exclusive skins, while another who engages in competitive play might be targeted with offers for performance-enhancing items.

Dynamic pricing is another area where AI can enhance monetisation. AI can adjust prices for in-game items based on factors such as player engagement, spending history, and market demand. This ensures that offers remain attractive and relevant, maximizing conversion rates.

AI can also optimize ad placement within games. By understanding player behavior and preferences, AI can determine the optimal moments and formats for displaying ads, minimizing disruption and enhancing ad effectiveness. For example, ads might be shown during natural pauses in gameplay or integrated seamlessly into the game environment.

Predictive analytics powered by AI can help developers anticipate market trends and player needs. By analyzing large datasets, AI can identify emerging patterns and preferences, allowing developers to adjust their monetisation strategies proactively. This includes predicting which new features or items will drive the most engagement and revenue.

Chatbots and virtual assistants powered by AI can enhance player support and engagement. These tools can provide real-time assistance, answer questions, and guide players through in-game purchases. By improving the overall player experience, AI-driven support can increase player satisfaction and retention.

AI-driven game design can also create more engaging and monetizable experiences. Procedural content generation, for example, allows for the creation of unique and personalized game worlds for each player. This keeps the game fresh and engaging, encouraging players to invest in the game over the long term.

However, the use of AI in monetisation raises ethical considerations. Ensuring transparency and fairness in AI-driven decisions is crucial to maintaining player trust. Developers must also be mindful of the potential for AI to exploit player vulnerabilities and design systems that prioritize player well-being.

As AI technology continues to evolve, it will play an increasingly central role in game monetisation. By leveraging AI to create personalized, adaptive, and engaging experiences, developers can drive revenue growth while enhancing player satisfaction.

12.4 Monetising Cross-Platform Play

Cross-platform play is becoming a standard feature in mobile gaming, allowing players to interact and compete across different devices and operating systems. Monetising cross-platform play presents unique opportunities and challenges for developers.

One of the primary benefits of cross-platform play is the expansion of the player base. By enabling players on mobile, console, and PC to play together, developers can reach a broader audience and increase engagement. This expanded player base enhances monetisation potential through a larger market for in-game purchases and ads.

Cross-platform play also encourages social interactions and community building. Players can connect with friends and other gamers regardless of their device, creating a more inclusive and engaging experience. Social features, such as cross-platform leaderboards and multiplayer modes, can drive player retention and spending.

Monetisation strategies for cross-platform play must consider the different spending behaviors and preferences of players on various devices. For example, console players might prefer purchasing premium content and expansions, while mobile players might favor microtransactions and ad-supported models. Developers need to offer a variety of monetisation options that cater to these diverse preferences.

Cross-platform play also allows for synchronized progression and purchases. Players can make in-game purchases on one device and access them on another, providing a seamless experience. This convenience encourages spending, as players can enjoy their purchases across multiple platforms.

Advertising in cross-platform games requires careful integration to avoid disrupting the player experience. Ads should be relevant and contextually appropriate for each platform. For example, mobile players might see rewarded video ads, while console players might encounter in-game sponsorships or branded content.

Developers must also address technical challenges associated with cross-platform play. Ensuring consistent performance and user experience across different devices is crucial. Cross-platform compatibility testing and optimization are essential to prevent issues that could negatively impact player satisfaction and monetisation.

Security and anti-cheat measures are critical in cross-platform games. Developers must implement robust systems to prevent cheating and hacking, which can undermine the game's integrity and drive players away. Fair and secure gameplay fosters a positive player experience and supports monetisation efforts.

Cross-platform play opens up new opportunities for collaborative events and promotions. Developers can host cross-platform tournaments, challenges, and special events that encourage participation and spending. These events can leverage the combined player base to create a sense of excitement and community.

As cross-platform play continues to gain popularity, developers must innovate and adapt their monetisation strategies to fully capitalize on its potential. By offering seamless and engaging experiences across different devices, developers can enhance player satisfaction and drive revenue growth.

12.5 Innovations in Mobile Game Monetisation

The mobile gaming industry is constantly evolving, with new innovations in monetisation strategies emerging to meet changing player preferences and market dynamics. Developers are exploring creative approaches to drive revenue while enhancing the player experience.

One significant innovation is the integration of augmented reality (AR) and virtual reality (VR) elements into mobile games. These technologies create immersive experiences that can be monetized through in-app purchases, subscriptions, and advertising. For example, AR games can offer virtual items that enhance real-world interactions, while VR games can provide premium content for more immersive experiences.

Blockchain technology is also revolutionizing mobile game monetisation. By enabling decentralized economies and true ownership of in-game assets through non-fungible tokens (NFTs), blockchain allows players to trade and sell virtual items. This creates new revenue streams for developers and increases player engagement by adding real-world value to in-game assets.

Subscription models are gaining popularity as players seek continuous access to premium content. Mobile games are offering subscription services that provide exclusive benefits, such as new levels, characters, and in-game currency. These models ensure a steady revenue stream and enhance player loyalty by offering ongoing value.

Personalization is another key trend in mobile game monetisation. By leveraging data analytics and artificial intelligence (AI), developers can offer personalized in-game offers and experiences tailored to individual player preferences. Personalized offers are more likely to convert, increasing revenue while providing a more satisfying player experience.

Ad-supported models are becoming more sophisticated, with non-intrusive and interactive ad formats gaining traction. Rewarded video ads, where players receive in-game rewards for watching ads, are particularly effective. Developers are also exploring native ads that blend seamlessly with the game environment, enhancing the player experience while generating ad revenue.

Live events and seasonal content are driving player engagement and monetisation. By introducing limited-time events, special challenges, and exclusive content, developers can create a sense of urgency and excitement. These events encourage players to spend on in-game items and participate actively, boosting both engagement and revenue.

Social features and community-building initiatives are enhancing monetisation strategies. Games that foster social interactions and community engagement see higher player retention and spending. Features such as multiplayer modes, social sharing, and in-game chat enhance the social experience, driving long-term engagement and monetisation.

Cross-promotion and collaborations with other brands and games are also emerging as effective monetisation strategies. Developers can partner with popular brands to introduce co-branded content and events, attracting new players and driving revenue. Cross-promotions with other games can leverage existing player bases, enhancing visibility and engagement.

THEORY AND IMPLEMENTATION DEVELOPMENT

As the mobile gaming industry continues to innovate, developers must stay agile and responsive to emerging trends and player preferences. By exploring new technologies, personalizing experiences, and fostering community engagement, developers can create effective monetisation strategies that drive sustainable revenue growth.

Chapter 13: Marketing and Monetisation

13.1 Marketing Strategies for Monetised Games

Effective marketing strategies are crucial for the success of monetised games. These strategies ensure that the game reaches the right audience and maximises revenue. Below are several key marketing strategies that can be employed.

One fundamental strategy is **identifying the target audience**. Knowing who the game is for helps in tailoring marketing messages and channels to reach potential players effectively. This involves understanding demographic details such as age, gender, location, and interests.

Utilising social media platforms is another critical strategy. Platforms like Facebook, Twitter, Instagram, and TikTok offer powerful tools for targeting specific audiences with advertisements. Social media also allows for organic marketing through community building and engagement.

Influencer partnerships can significantly boost a game's visibility. By collaborating with influencers who have a substantial following, game developers can tap into new audiences. Influencers can provide reviews, gameplay demonstrations, and endorsements that resonate well with their followers.

Content marketing through blogs, videos, and tutorials helps in educating potential players about the game. High-quality content can improve SEO rankings and drive organic traffic to the game's website or app store page. Consistent content updates keep the audience engaged and informed.

Email marketing remains a robust tool for engagement. By building an email list, developers can send out newsletters, updates, and promotional offers directly to interested users. Personalized emails with targeted offers can enhance user retention and monetisation.

In-game events and promotions are effective in retaining players and driving spending. Special events, seasonal updates, and limited-time offers create urgency and excitement, encouraging players to spend more time and money in the game.

App store optimization (ASO) is essential for improving the visibility of a game in app stores. This involves optimizing the game's title, description, keywords, and visuals to ensure it ranks higher in search results and attracts more downloads.

Paid advertising campaigns on platforms like Google Ads, Facebook Ads, and mobile ad networks can drive significant traffic to the game. These campaigns should be carefully managed to ensure a high return on investment (ROI).

Community management plays a crucial role in building a loyal player base. Engaging with the community through forums, social media, and in-game chats fosters a sense of belonging and loyalty, which can translate into increased spending.

A/B testing different marketing approaches helps in understanding what resonates best with the audience. By testing various elements such as ad creatives, landing pages, and call-to-action buttons, developers can optimize their marketing strategies for better performance.

Data analytics is vital for measuring the effectiveness of marketing campaigns. Tools like Google Analytics, Facebook Insights, and in-game analytics provide valuable data on user behavior and campaign performance. This data can be used to refine and improve marketing efforts.

Cross-promotion with other games or brands can expand reach and attract new players. Collaborative promotions can leverage the strengths of both parties and create mutually beneficial outcomes.

Public relations (PR) efforts, including press releases, media coverage, and interviews, help in building a positive image and increasing awareness about the game. A strong PR strategy can complement other marketing efforts and enhance credibility.

Localisation of marketing materials is crucial for reaching international audiences. Translating and culturally adapting content ensures that marketing messages resonate with players from different regions.

Utilising user-generated content (UGC), such as fan art, videos, and reviews, can enhance authenticity and engagement. Encouraging players to create and share content related to the game builds a sense of community and loyalty.

Rewarding loyal players through loyalty programs, VIP memberships, and exclusive content can enhance retention and spending. Recognizing and rewarding players' dedication fosters a positive relationship and encourages continued engagement.

Analyzing competitor strategies provides insights into what works in the market. By studying successful competitors, developers can adopt best practices and avoid common pitfalls.

Continuous optimization of marketing strategies is necessary to adapt to changing trends and player preferences. Regularly reviewing and updating marketing plans ensures sustained success and growth.

In conclusion, a multifaceted marketing approach is essential for the successful monetisation of mobile games. By employing a combination of these strategies, developers can effectively reach and engage their target audience, driving both user acquisition and revenue growth.

13.2 Leveraging Social Media for Monetisation

Chapter 13: Marketing and Monetisation

Social media has become an indispensable tool for mobile game monetisation. Its vast reach and engagement capabilities make it ideal for promoting games and driving player spending. Here are several ways to leverage social media for monetisation.

Creating engaging content is the foundation of any successful social media strategy. Content should be visually appealing, informative, and relevant to the target audience. This includes game trailers, teasers, behind-the-scenes looks, and player testimonials.

Regular posting keeps the audience engaged and informed about updates, events, and promotions. A consistent posting schedule helps maintain visibility and keeps the game top-of-mind for followers.

Interactive posts such as polls, quizzes, and contests encourage engagement and create a sense of community. These activities can also provide valuable insights into player preferences and behaviors.

Live streaming on platforms like Twitch, YouTube, and Facebook Live offers real-time interaction with players. Live streams can include gameplay demonstrations, Q&A sessions, and live events, creating excitement and driving engagement.

Social media advertising allows for precise targeting of potential players. Platforms like Facebook and Instagram offer robust advertising tools that can target users based on demographics, interests, and behaviors. This ensures that marketing efforts reach the most relevant audience.

Influencer collaborations can amplify reach and credibility. Partnering with popular influencers who have a significant following can introduce the game to new audiences and build trust through authentic endorsements.

User-generated content campaigns encourage players to create and share their own content related to the game. This not only increases engagement but also provides social proof, as potential players see real people enjoying the game.

Utilizing social media analytics helps in understanding what content performs best. Metrics such as likes, shares, comments, and click-through rates provide insights into audience preferences and the effectiveness of marketing efforts.

Running exclusive promotions and giveaways on social media can boost engagement and attract new players. Limited-time offers, discount codes, and in-game rewards create a sense of urgency and encourage followers to take action.

Building a community through dedicated groups or forums fosters a sense of belonging among players. These communities can become self-sustaining, with players helping each other and promoting the game organically.

Sharing player achievements and milestones recognizes and rewards players, enhancing their loyalty and encouraging continued engagement. Highlighting top players or notable accomplishments fosters a competitive and engaged community.

Cross-promoting content across different social media platforms maximizes reach. Content can be repurposed and tailored for each platform to ensure it resonates with the specific audience there.

Engaging with followers by responding to comments, messages, and mentions builds a positive relationship with the community. Active engagement shows that the developers value player feedback and are committed to improving the game experience.

Hosting virtual events and tournaments on social media can drive engagement and spending. These events create excitement and provide opportunities for players to compete and interact with each other.

Collaborating with other brands or games for joint promotions can expand reach and attract new players. Cross-promotions leverage the strengths of both parties and can introduce the game to new audiences.

Monitoring social media trends and adapting content accordingly keeps the game relevant and engaging. Staying on top of trends ensures that marketing efforts remain fresh and resonate with the audience.

Providing exclusive content or early access to social media followers creates a sense of exclusivity and rewards loyalty. This can include sneak peeks, beta tests, or special in-game items available only to followers.

Encouraging social sharing of game-related content can expand reach organically. Players sharing their achievements, game moments, or promotional content with their networks can drive word-of-mouth marketing.

Utilizing hashtags and keywords effectively increases the visibility of posts. Relevant hashtags and keywords help in reaching a broader audience and ensuring that content is discoverable.

In conclusion, leveraging social media for monetisation involves a combination of engaging content, targeted advertising, influencer collaborations, and active community management. By effectively utilizing these strategies, developers can maximize their reach, engage their audience, and drive player spending.

13.3 Influencer and Affiliate Marketing

Influencer and affiliate marketing have become powerful tools in promoting mobile games and driving monetisation. These strategies leverage the reach and credibility of influencers and affiliates to attract new players and boost revenue. Here are several ways to implement effective influencer and affiliate marketing.

Identifying the right influencers is crucial for a successful campaign. Influencers should have a substantial following that matches the game's target audience. This ensures that the promotional content reaches potential players who are likely to be interested in the game.

Building relationships with influencers involves more than just transactional agreements. Engaging with influencers on a personal level, understanding their content style, and providing them with early access to the game can lead to more authentic and enthusiastic endorsements.

Providing influencers with creative freedom allows them to promote the game in a way that resonates with their audience. Influencers know their followers best and can create content that is both engaging and persuasive.

Offering exclusive content or early access to influencers can generate buzz and anticipation among their followers. Exclusive previews, special in-game items, or early access to new features can make the promotion more enticing.

Tracking the performance of influencer campaigns through unique links or discount codes helps in measuring their effectiveness. This data can provide insights into which influencers drive the most traffic and conversions, allowing for better optimization of future campaigns.

Affiliate marketing programs involve partnering with individuals or companies who promote the game in exchange for a commission on sales or in-game purchases. Affiliates can include bloggers, website owners, and social media personalities.

Setting up an affiliate program involves creating a system for tracking referrals and calculating commissions. There are various affiliate marketing platforms that can help manage these aspects efficiently.

Providing affiliates with marketing materials such as banners, text links, and social media posts makes it easier for them to promote the game. High-quality and engaging materials increase the likelihood of attracting potential players.

Offering competitive commissions can attract top-tier affiliates who have a significant reach and influence. A well-structured commission plan motivates affiliates to promote the game more actively.

Regularly communicating with affiliates helps in maintaining strong relationships and ensuring they have the support they need. Providing updates, sharing best practices, and recognizing top performers can foster loyalty and commitment.

Utilizing affiliate networks can expand the reach of the affiliate program. These networks connect developers with a large pool of potential affiliates, making it easier to scale the program and reach new audiences.

Creating a tiered affiliate program can incentivize affiliates to achieve higher performance levels. Offering higher commissions or additional rewards for top performers can motivate affiliates to increase their promotional efforts.

Monitoring and analyzing affiliate performance is crucial for optimizing the program. Using analytics tools to track clicks, conversions, and revenue generated by affiliates helps in identifying which partners are most effective and why.

Combining influencer and affiliate marketing strategies can amplify the impact of promotional efforts. Influencers can be part of the affiliate program, earning commissions on the traffic and sales they generate, creating a win-win situation for both parties.

Providing clear guidelines and support to influencers and affiliates ensures that they understand the game's key features and selling points. This helps in creating consistent and accurate promotional content.

Hosting joint events or streams with influencers can create a more interactive and engaging promotional experience. These events can include Q&A sessions, gameplay demonstrations, and live competitions, attracting more viewers and potential players.

Leveraging user-generated content created by influencers and affiliates can enhance credibility and reach. Sharing this content on the game's official channels can amplify its impact and build trust with potential players.

Offering special promotions or bonuses to players referred by influencers and affiliates can increase conversions. Limited-time offers, exclusive in-game items, or discount codes can incentivize potential players to try the game.

Regularly reviewing and optimizing influencer and affiliate marketing strategies ensures that they remain effective and aligned with the game's goals. Continuous improvement based on performance data helps in maximizing the return on investment.

In conclusion, influencer and affiliate marketing are powerful strategies for promoting mobile games and driving monetisation. By building strong relationships, providing creative freedom, and offering competitive incentives, developers can effectively leverage the reach and credibility of influencers and affiliates to attract new players and boost revenue.

13.4 Launch and Post-Launch Marketing

The launch and post-launch phases are critical for the success of a mobile game. Effective marketing strategies during these periods can significantly impact player acquisition, retention, and monetisation. Here are several key approaches for launch and post-launch marketing.

Pre-launch marketing involves building anticipation and excitement before the game's release. This can be achieved through teaser campaigns, countdowns, and sneak peeks. Creating a sense of anticipation can drive initial downloads and engagement.

Beta testing and soft launches allow for gathering feedback and making improvements before the full release. Inviting a select group of players to test the game helps in identifying issues and optimizing the gameplay experience.

Press releases and media coverage can generate buzz and attract attention from potential players. Reaching out to gaming publications, blogs, and influencers with press kits and review copies can lead to valuable coverage and reviews.

Social media campaigns should be ramped up during the launch period. Engaging content, live streams, and interactive posts can attract attention and drive downloads. Utilizing hashtags and trending topics can increase visibility.

App store optimization (ASO) is crucial for maximizing visibility in app stores. This involves optimizing the game's title, description, keywords, and visuals to ensure it ranks higher in search results and attracts more downloads.

Paid advertising campaigns can drive significant traffic during the launch phase. Platforms like Google Ads, Facebook Ads, and mobile ad networks offer targeted advertising options that can reach potential players effectively.

Influencer partnerships during the launch can amplify reach and credibility. Influencers can create launch day content, live streams, and reviews that introduce the game to their followers and encourage downloads.

Community engagement is essential for building a loyal player base. Engaging with players on social media, forums, and in-game chats fosters a sense of belonging and encourages word-of-mouth marketing.

Post-launch updates and content keep players engaged and coming back for more. Regular updates with new features, events, and content can maintain interest and drive continued engagement and spending.

Analyzing launch performance through data analytics provides insights into what worked and what didn't. Metrics such as downloads, retention rates, and revenue help in understanding the effectiveness of launch strategies and identifying areas for improvement.

Engaging with player feedback is crucial for making post-launch improvements. Listening to player suggestions and addressing issues demonstrates a commitment to quality and can enhance player satisfaction and loyalty.

Hosting in-game events and promotions can boost post-launch engagement and spending. Limited-time events, special rewards, and seasonal updates create excitement and encourage players to stay active.

Cross-promotions with other games or brands can expand reach and attract new players. Collaborative promotions leverage the strengths of both parties and introduce the game to new audiences.

Maintaining a strong online presence through regular content updates, blog posts, and social media activity keeps the game top-of-mind for players. Consistent engagement ensures that players remain interested and informed about new developments.

Offering loyalty rewards and incentives to early adopters and loyal players can enhance retention. Recognizing and rewarding dedicated players fosters a positive relationship and encourages continued engagement and spending.

Implementing retention strategies such as push notifications, email campaigns, and in-game reminders helps in keeping players engaged. Personalized messages and offers can re-engage inactive players and drive them back to the game.

Monitoring competitor activities provides insights into market trends and best practices. Understanding what works for successful competitors can inform and improve post-launch strategies.

Adapting to player behavior and preferences is crucial for long-term success. Continuous monitoring and analysis of player data help in making informed decisions about updates, content, and monetisation strategies.

Building long-term relationships with players through community management and regular engagement ensures sustained interest and loyalty. Active communication and support demonstrate a commitment to the player community.

In conclusion, effective launch and post-launch marketing strategies are essential for the success of a mobile game. By building anticipation, engaging with players, and continuously optimizing strategies based on data and feedback, developers can maximize player acquisition, retention, and monetisation.

13.5 Measuring Marketing Effectiveness

Measuring the effectiveness of marketing efforts is crucial for optimizing strategies and ensuring the success of a mobile game. Several key metrics and analytical tools can help in evaluating the impact of marketing campaigns and making informed decisions. Here are several approaches to measuring marketing effectiveness.

Key Performance Indicators (KPIs) are essential for tracking the success of marketing efforts. Common KPIs for mobile games include downloads, active users, retention rates, in-app purchases, and revenue. These metrics provide a clear picture of the game's performance and the effectiveness of marketing strategies.

User acquisition cost (UAC) measures the cost of acquiring a new player. This includes expenses related to advertising, influencer partnerships, and other marketing activities. Lowering the UAC while maintaining or increasing the number of new players is a key goal.

Return on investment (ROI) evaluates the profitability of marketing campaigns. By comparing the revenue generated from new players to the cost of acquiring them, developers can assess the financial success of their marketing efforts.

Lifetime value (LTV) of a player estimates the total revenue generated by a player over their entire engagement with the game. Comparing the LTV to the UAC helps in understanding the long-term profitability of marketing strategies.

Conversion rates measure the percentage of players who take a desired action, such as downloading the game, making an in-app purchase, or engaging with a promotion. High conversion rates indicate effective marketing efforts and player interest.

Engagement metrics such as session length, session frequency, and in-game actions provide insights into player behavior and satisfaction. High engagement levels often correlate with better retention and monetisation.

Churn rate measures the percentage of players who stop playing the game over a specific period. Reducing churn is essential for maintaining a stable player base and maximizing revenue.

Funnel analysis tracks the player's journey from initial exposure to the game to making a purchase or other desired actions. Identifying drop-off points in the funnel helps in optimizing the user experience and improving conversion rates.

A/B testing involves comparing different versions of marketing materials, such as ad creatives, landing pages, and call-to-action buttons, to determine which performs better. This helps in refining marketing strategies based on empirical data.

Social media analytics provide insights into the reach, engagement, and effectiveness of social media campaigns. Metrics such as likes, shares, comments, and click-through rates help in understanding audience behavior and preferences.

Attribution models assign credit to different marketing touchpoints that contribute to a player's conversion. Understanding which channels and campaigns drive the most conversions helps in allocating marketing budgets more effectively.

Surveys and feedback from players can provide qualitative insights into the effectiveness of marketing efforts. Direct feedback from players helps in understanding their motivations, preferences, and perceptions of the game.

Competitor analysis provides benchmarks for evaluating the success of marketing strategies. Comparing the game's performance to similar games in the market helps in identifying strengths and areas for improvement.

Cohort analysis groups players based on specific characteristics or behaviors and tracks their performance over time. This helps in understanding how different segments of the player base respond to marketing efforts.

Marketing dashboards consolidate data from various sources and provide a comprehensive view of marketing performance. These dashboards can include real-time updates on key metrics, making it easier to monitor and optimize campaigns.

Retention metrics such as day-1, day-7, and day-30 retention rates provide insights into how well the game retains players over time. High retention rates indicate a successful onboarding process and engaging gameplay.

Predictive analytics use historical data to forecast future trends and player behavior. These insights help in making proactive decisions about marketing strategies and resource allocation.

Ad performance metrics such as click-through rates (CTR), cost per click (CPC), and cost per thousand impressions (CPM) provide insights into the effectiveness of advertising campaigns. Optimizing these metrics helps in maximizing the impact of ad spend.

Cross-channel analytics track player interactions across different marketing channels. Understanding how players move between social media, email, in-game notifications, and other channels helps in creating cohesive and effective marketing campaigns.

In conclusion, measuring marketing effectiveness involves a combination of quantitative and qualitative metrics. By regularly tracking and analyzing these metrics, developers can optimize their marketing strategies, improve player acquisition and retention, and maximize revenue.

Chapter 14: Case Studies of Successful Mobile Games

14.1 Analysis of Top-Grossing Mobile Games

Analyzing top-grossing mobile games provides valuable insights into successful monetisation strategies. By examining what works for these games, developers can learn best practices and apply similar tactics to their own projects. Here are several key aspects of top-grossing mobile games.

Robust monetisation models are a hallmark of successful games. These games often employ a combination of monetisation strategies, such as in-app purchases, ads, and subscriptions, to maximize revenue. A well-balanced approach ensures multiple revenue streams and reduces reliance on a single source.

Engaging gameplay mechanics are essential for retaining players and encouraging spending. Top-grossing games often feature addictive and enjoyable gameplay that keeps players coming back. This includes rewarding progression systems, challenging levels, and engaging narratives.

Frequent updates and new content keep the game fresh and exciting. Regular updates with new features, levels, and events maintain player interest and drive continued engagement. This approach ensures that players have something new to look forward to and are more likely to spend money.

Effective use of data analytics helps in understanding player behavior and optimizing the game experience. Top-grossing games use analytics to track key metrics, such as player retention, spending patterns, and engagement levels. This data informs decisions about updates, monetisation, and marketing strategies.

Strong community engagement builds a loyal player base. Successful games often have active communities on social media, forums, and in-game chats. Engaging with players, responding to feedback, and fostering a sense of community enhances player loyalty and encourages word-of-mouth marketing.

High-quality graphics and design contribute to an immersive gaming experience. Top-grossing games often invest in stunning visuals, smooth animations, and intuitive user interfaces. A polished and visually appealing game attracts and retains players more effectively.

Strategic marketing campaigns drive player acquisition and retention. These games often employ a mix of paid advertising, influencer partnerships, and social media campaigns to reach a broad audience. Effective marketing ensures that the game reaches its target players and maintains visibility.

Balanced in-game economy is crucial for sustainable monetisation. Successful games carefully design their in-game economies to ensure that players feel motivated to spend without feeling pressured or frustrated. This involves setting fair prices for virtual goods and offering meaningful rewards.

Localized content and marketing help in reaching global audiences. Top-grossing games often localize their content, marketing materials, and customer support to cater to different regions. This approach ensures that the game resonates with players from diverse cultural backgrounds.

Compelling narratives and characters enhance player engagement. Games with strong stories and relatable characters create emotional connections with players. These connections increase player investment in the game and drive spending on in-game items and content.

Seasonal and limited-time events create excitement and urgency. Special events, seasonal updates, and time-limited offers encourage players to log in regularly and spend money. These events create a dynamic game environment that keeps players engaged.

Cross-promotion with other games or brands can expand reach and attract new players. Successful games often collaborate with other popular games, brands, or franchises to introduce new content and attract fans from different communities.

Incentivizing player referrals can drive organic growth. Top-grossing games often implement referral programs that reward players for inviting friends to join the game. These programs leverage existing player networks to attract new users.

Optimizing onboarding processes ensures that new players have a positive initial experience. Successful games focus on creating smooth and engaging onboarding experiences that introduce players to the game's mechanics and features. A strong start increases the likelihood of long-term engagement.

Personalized experiences enhance player satisfaction. Top-grossing games often use data analytics to tailor the game experience to individual players. Personalized offers, recommendations, and content make players feel valued and increase their likelihood of spending.

Building long-term player loyalty through consistent engagement and rewards is key. Successful games focus on retaining players by offering loyalty rewards, exclusive content, and ongoing support. Long-term loyalty translates to sustained revenue and a stable player base.

Implementing feedback loops ensures continuous improvement. Top-grossing games actively seek and incorporate player feedback to improve the game. Regular updates and improvements based on feedback demonstrate a commitment to quality and player satisfaction.

Leveraging technological advancements keeps the game competitive. Successful games often adopt new technologies, such as AR, VR, or blockchain, to enhance the player experience and offer unique features. Staying ahead of technological trends ensures continued player interest.

Monitoring and adapting to market trends is essential for staying relevant. Top-grossing games continuously analyze market trends and adapt their strategies to meet changing player preferences and industry dynamics. This proactive approach ensures sustained success.

In conclusion, analyzing top-grossing mobile games reveals several best practices that contribute to their success. By adopting robust monetisation models, engaging gameplay mechanics, effective marketing strategies, and strong community engagement, developers can create successful and profitable mobile games.

14.2 Lessons from Successful Monetisation Strategies

Successful monetisation strategies from top-grossing mobile games offer valuable lessons for other developers. By understanding and implementing these strategies, developers can enhance their own monetisation efforts and maximize revenue. Here are several key lessons from successful monetisation strategies.

Diversifying revenue streams is crucial for stability and growth. Top-grossing games often employ multiple monetisation methods, such as in-app purchases, ads, subscriptions, and premium content. Diversification reduces reliance on a single revenue source and maximizes overall earnings.

Creating a balanced in-game economy ensures sustainable monetisation. Successful games carefully design their economies to offer meaningful rewards, fair pricing, and progression incentives. A well-balanced economy encourages spending without frustrating players.

Implementing a fair and transparent monetisation model builds player trust. Top-grossing games are upfront about their monetisation methods and ensure that players understand what they are paying for. Transparency reduces the risk of backlash and enhances player satisfaction.

Offering value through in-app purchases is essential for driving spending. Successful games provide in-app purchases that offer real value to players, such as exclusive items, faster progression, and enhanced gameplay experiences. Value-driven purchases are more likely to be embraced by players.

Utilizing data analytics helps in optimizing monetisation strategies. Top-grossing games use data to track player behavior, spending patterns, and engagement levels. This data informs decisions about pricing, promotions, and new content, ensuring that monetisation efforts are effective.

Regularly updating the game with new content keeps players engaged and spending. Successful games frequently introduce new features, levels, events, and items to maintain player interest. Regular updates create a dynamic game environment that encourages ongoing engagement and spending.

Personalizing offers and promotions enhances player satisfaction. Top-grossing games use player data to tailor offers and promotions to individual players. Personalized offers make players feel valued and increase the likelihood of spending.

Incorporating limited-time events and promotions creates urgency and excitement. Special events, seasonal updates, and time-limited offers encourage players to spend money to take advantage of exclusive opportunities. These events drive short-term spending and long-term engagement.

Building a strong community fosters loyalty and long-term monetisation. Successful games engage with their communities through social media, forums, and in-game chats. Active community engagement creates a sense of belonging and encourages players to invest in the game.

Rewarding player loyalty through exclusive content and perks enhances retention. Top-grossing games often offer loyalty programs, VIP memberships, and exclusive rewards for dedicated players. Recognizing and rewarding loyalty fosters long-term engagement and spending.

Optimizing the onboarding process ensures a positive initial experience for new players. Successful games focus on creating smooth and engaging onboarding experiences that introduce players to the game's mechanics and features. A strong start increases the likelihood of long-term engagement and spending.

Leveraging influencer partnerships can amplify reach and credibility. Collaborating with influencers who resonate with the target audience can introduce the game to new players and build trust through authentic endorsements. Influencers can drive significant traffic and conversions.

Utilizing social proof and user-generated content builds credibility. Top-grossing games often highlight positive reviews, player testimonials, and user-generated content. Social proof reassures potential players and encourages them to try the game and spend money.

Implementing a robust retention strategy is essential for sustained monetisation. Successful games use push notifications, email campaigns, and in-game reminders to keep players engaged. Retention strategies ensure that players continue to return and spend money over time.

Adapting to player feedback demonstrates a commitment to quality and player satisfaction. Top-grossing games actively seek and incorporate player feedback to improve the game. Regular updates and improvements based on feedback enhance player loyalty and spending.

Exploring new technologies and trends keeps the game competitive. Successful games often adopt new technologies, such as AR, VR, or blockchain, to enhance the player experience and offer unique features. Staying ahead of technological trends ensures continued player interest and spending.

Monitoring competitor strategies provides valuable insights. Analyzing successful competitors helps in understanding what works in the market and adopting best practices. Competitor analysis informs decisions about monetisation, marketing, and game design.

Continuously optimizing monetisation strategies is crucial for long-term success. Top-grossing games regularly review and refine their monetisation efforts based on data and market trends. Continuous optimization ensures sustained revenue and growth.

In conclusion, successful monetisation strategies from top-grossing mobile games offer valuable lessons for other developers. By diversifying revenue streams, creating a balanced in-game economy, leveraging data analytics, and engaging with the community, developers can enhance their own monetisation efforts and maximize revenue.

14.3 Failures and What They Teach Us

While successful mobile games provide valuable lessons, failures also offer critical insights. Understanding the reasons behind the failure of certain games can help developers avoid common pitfalls and improve their own projects. Here are several key lessons from failed mobile games.

Over-reliance on a single monetisation method can lead to failure. Games that rely solely on one revenue stream, such as ads or in-app purchases, may struggle to sustain revenue. Diversifying monetisation methods ensures multiple income sources and reduces risk.

Poorly balanced in-game economy can frustrate players and drive them away. Games with unfair pricing, excessive paywalls, or unbalanced progression systems can lead to player dissatisfaction. A well-designed economy is crucial for player retention and monetisation.

Lack of regular updates and new content can result in player attrition. Games that fail to introduce fresh content, features, and events may lose player interest. Regular updates keep the game dynamic and engaging, encouraging ongoing player involvement.

Ignoring player feedback can lead to negative reviews and decreased engagement. Games that do not address player concerns or implement feedback may face backlash and declining player numbers. Actively listening to and incorporating player feedback is essential.

Inadequate onboarding processes can result in poor retention rates. Games that do not effectively introduce new players to the gameplay and mechanics may struggle to retain them. A smooth and engaging onboarding experience is crucial for retaining new players.

Excessive monetisation pressure can alienate players. Games that aggressively push in-app purchases or ads can frustrate players and lead to negative perceptions. Balancing monetisation with a positive player experience is essential for long-term success.

Failing to build a community can result in low player engagement. Games that do not foster a sense of community may struggle to retain players. Engaging with players through social media, forums, and in-game chats builds loyalty and encourages word-of-mouth marketing.

Lack of effective marketing can hinder player acquisition. Games that do not invest in marketing efforts may struggle to reach their target audience. A robust marketing strategy is crucial for attracting new players and driving downloads.

Ignoring market trends can result in outdated gameplay and features. Games that do not adapt to changing player preferences and industry trends may become irrelevant. Staying informed about market trends and incorporating new technologies keeps the game competitive.

Poor technical performance and bugs can drive players away. Games that suffer from frequent crashes, lag, or bugs can frustrate players and lead to negative reviews. Ensuring technical stability and addressing issues promptly is crucial for player retention.

Inadequate customer support can result in negative player experiences. Games that do not provide timely and effective support may lose players who encounter issues. Strong customer support enhances player satisfaction and loyalty.

Ignoring localization can limit the game's global reach. Games that do not localize content, marketing materials, and customer support may struggle to attract players from different regions. Localization ensures that the game resonates with a diverse audience.

Lack of clear goals and direction can lead to unfocused development and marketing efforts. Games that do not have a clear vision or strategy may struggle to attract and retain players. Setting clear goals and maintaining focus is essential for success.

Inadequate data analysis can result in missed opportunities and poor decision-making. Games that do not leverage data analytics to track player behavior, spending patterns, and engagement levels may struggle to optimize their strategies. Data-driven decision-making is crucial for success.

Failing to differentiate from competitors can result in low player interest. Games that do not offer unique features or a compelling value proposition may struggle to stand out in a crowded market. Differentiation is key to attracting and retaining players.

Underestimating the importance of user experience (UX) can result in poor player satisfaction. Games that do not prioritize UX may frustrate players with confusing interfaces, difficult navigation, or poor design. A positive UX is essential for player retention and engagement.

Ignoring ethical considerations can lead to player backlash. Games that employ manipulative or unethical monetisation practices may face negative reviews and decreased player trust. Ethical considerations are crucial for maintaining a positive reputation and player satisfaction.

Failing to adapt and iterate can result in stagnation. Games that do not continuously improve and adapt to player feedback and market trends may struggle to maintain relevance. Iterative development ensures that the game evolves and remains engaging.

Overestimating initial success can lead to complacency. Games that achieve early success but do not continue to innovate and improve may see declining player numbers. Sustained success requires ongoing effort and adaptation.

In conclusion, failures in mobile game development offer valuable lessons for avoiding common pitfalls. By diversifying revenue streams, balancing the in-game economy, actively engaging with players, and continuously improving the game, developers can enhance their chances of success and avoid the mistakes that have led to the failure of other games.

14.4 Evolution of Monetisation in Iconic Games

The evolution of monetisation strategies in iconic mobile games provides valuable insights into the industry's development and best practices. By examining how successful games have adapted their monetisation approaches over time, developers can learn important lessons for their own projects. Here are several key examples of the evolution of monetisation in iconic games.

Angry Birds initially launched as a paid game, but later transitioned to a freemium model. The game introduced in-app purchases for power-ups and additional content, significantly increasing its revenue. This shift highlights the potential of freemium models in maximizing earnings.

Candy Crush Saga revolutionized the freemium model with its "lives" system, where players could purchase extra lives or wait for them to regenerate. This approach created a recurring revenue stream and encouraged regular player engagement. The introduction of new levels and events kept the game fresh and maintained player interest.

Clash of Clans implemented a hybrid monetisation model, combining in-app purchases with ads. Players could buy gems to speed up progression or watch ads for smaller rewards. This dual approach diversified revenue streams and catered to different player preferences. Regular updates and seasonal events further enhanced monetisation.

Pokémon GO utilized location-based monetisation strategies, partnering with real-world businesses for sponsored locations. This innovative approach generated revenue from both players and business partners. In-app purchases for items and event tickets provided additional income. The game's success demonstrated the potential of integrating real-world elements into mobile gaming.

Fortnite introduced a battle pass system, offering players a seasonal subscription for exclusive content and rewards. This model encouraged regular engagement and spending, as players aimed to complete challenges and unlock rewards. The game's monetisation strategy evolved to include in-game concerts and collaborations with popular brands, further driving revenue.

Hearthstone employed a card pack system, where players could purchase packs to collect cards and build decks. The introduction of expansion packs and limited-time events kept the game engaging and monetisation strong. Regular balance updates and new content ensured long-term player retention and spending.

PUBG Mobile adopted a tiered monetisation approach, offering in-game purchases, a battle pass, and ad-supported rewards. This combination catered to different player preferences and maximized revenue potential. Seasonal updates, new game modes, and collaborations with popular franchises kept the game relevant and engaging.

Roblox created a platform for user-generated content, allowing players to purchase virtual currency (Robux) to buy items and experiences. The introduction of premium memberships and developer payouts incentivized content creation and increased overall revenue. This model demonstrated the potential of community-driven monetisation.

Monument Valley initially launched as a premium game but later introduced paid expansions. This approach allowed the game to generate additional revenue while maintaining a premium experience. The success of Monument Valley highlighted the viability of paid expansions for premium games.

Genshin Impact combined gacha mechanics with a vast open-world experience. Players could spend money on wishes to obtain new characters and weapons. The game's monetisation strategy focused on regular updates, limited-time events, and character banners to drive spending. Genshin Impact's success demonstrated the potential of combining high-quality gameplay with gacha mechanics.

Among Us initially launched as a premium game but shifted to a free-to-play model with in-app purchases for cosmetic items. The introduction of new maps, game modes, and community-driven content kept the game engaging and monetisation strong. Among Us's success highlighted the potential of community-driven growth and monetisation.

Clash Royale introduced a card-based progression system, where players could purchase chests to obtain cards and upgrade their decks. Regular balance updates, new cards, and seasonal events kept the game engaging and monetisation strong. Clash Royale's success demonstrated the potential of combining strategic gameplay with monetisation.

Brawl Stars employed a similar monetisation approach to Clash Royale, with a focus on brawl boxes and in-game purchases. The introduction of new brawlers, game modes, and seasonal events kept the game engaging and monetisation strong. Brawl Stars's success highlighted the importance of regular updates and diverse content.

League of Legends: Wild Rift adapted the successful monetisation model of its PC counterpart, offering in-game purchases for champions and cosmetic items. The introduction of seasonal events, limited-time modes, and collaborations with popular franchises kept the game engaging and monetisation strong.

In conclusion, the evolution of monetisation strategies in iconic mobile games provides valuable insights into best practices and innovative approaches. By examining how successful games have adapted their monetisation models over time, developers can learn important lessons and apply similar tactics to their own projects.

14.5 Future Trends Predicted by Case Studies

Analyzing case studies of successful mobile games provides insights into future trends in game monetisation. By understanding current strategies and anticipating industry shifts, developers can stay ahead of the curve and maximize revenue opportunities. Here are several future trends predicted by case studies of successful mobile games.

Integration of blockchain technology is expected to revolutionize game monetisation. Blockchain can enable true ownership of in-game assets, allowing players to buy, sell, and trade items securely. This trend is already being explored by games like Axie Infinity and is likely to become more widespread.

Expansion of subscription models is anticipated as more games adopt battle passes and premium memberships. These models offer recurring revenue and encourage regular player engagement. The success of games like Fortnite and Roblox indicates a growing acceptance of subscription-based monetisation.

Increased use of augmented reality (AR) in games is expected to drive new monetisation opportunities. AR can create immersive experiences and real-world interactions, opening up possibilities for location-based monetisation and sponsored events. Pokémon GO's success with AR demonstrates its potential.

Personalized monetisation strategies will become more prevalent as data analytics and machine learning improve. Games will increasingly tailor offers, rewards, and content to individual players based on their behavior and preferences. Personalized experiences can enhance player satisfaction and spending.

Growth of cross-platform play will drive new monetisation strategies. As more games become available across multiple platforms, developers can create unified economies and experiences. Cross-platform play encourages broader player engagement and opens up new revenue streams.

Expansion of esports and competitive gaming is likely to drive monetisation through sponsorships, advertising, and premium content. Games like Clash Royale and Fortnite have successfully integrated esports, and this trend is expected to grow. Competitive gaming creates opportunities for new revenue streams and player engagement.

Social and community-driven monetisation will continue to evolve. Games that foster strong communities and social interactions will find new ways to monetize these relationships. User-generated content, community events, and social features will play a significant role in future monetisation strategies.

Emphasis on ethical monetisation will become increasingly important as players demand transparency and fairness. Developers will need to balance monetisation with player satisfaction, avoiding manipulative tactics and ensuring value-driven purchases. Ethical considerations will enhance long-term player loyalty.

Adoption of cloud gaming will drive changes in monetisation models. As cloud gaming becomes more popular, games will need to adapt their monetisation strategies to this new distribution method. Subscription-based models and streaming services will play a significant role in cloud gaming monetisation.

Introduction of AI-driven content generation will create new monetisation opportunities. AI can generate personalized content, levels, and challenges, keeping the game experience fresh and engaging. This can enhance player retention and spending by continuously offering new experiences.

Leveraging big data for predictive analytics will enable more effective monetisation strategies. By analyzing large datasets, developers can predict player behavior and optimize monetisation efforts. Predictive analytics will help in creating targeted offers and maximizing revenue.

Enhanced virtual reality (VR) experiences will drive new monetisation opportunities. As VR technology advances, games will offer more immersive and interactive experiences. VR can enable unique monetisation methods, such as virtual real estate, premium experiences, and exclusive content.

Expansion of influencer and affiliate marketing will continue to grow. Influencers and affiliates will play a significant role in promoting games and driving player acquisition. Collaborative promotions, sponsorships, and content partnerships will enhance monetisation efforts.

Focus on sustainability and social responsibility will influence monetisation strategies. Players are increasingly aware of environmental and social issues, and games that align with these values will attract positive attention. Sustainable practices and social responsibility will become important aspects of monetisation.

Globalization and localization will drive monetisation in diverse markets. As mobile games reach a global audience, developers will need to adapt their strategies to different cultural preferences and economic conditions. Localization will ensure that monetisation efforts resonate with players worldwide.

In conclusion, analyzing case studies of successful mobile games provides valuable insights into future trends in game monetisation. By anticipating these trends and adapting their strategies, developers can stay ahead of the curve and maximize revenue opportunities in an evolving industry.

Chapter 15: Player Feedback and Community Management

15.1 Importance of Player Feedback in Monetisation

Player feedback is crucial in shaping effective monetisation strategies in mobile games. By understanding player preferences and pain points, developers can make informed decisions that enhance the player experience and increase revenue. Feedback provides insights into what players value, enabling the creation of more appealing virtual goods, pricing strategies, and game features.

Engaging with player feedback helps in identifying potential issues before they escalate, allowing developers to address concerns promptly. This proactive approach not only improves player satisfaction but also fosters loyalty, which is essential for long-term monetisation. Regularly collecting and analyzing feedback ensures that the game evolves in line with player expectations, maintaining its relevance in a competitive market.

Incorporating feedback into game updates demonstrates to players that their opinions matter, building a sense of community and trust. This engagement can lead to higher retention rates, as players are more likely to stay invested in a game where they feel heard and valued. Moreover, satisfied players are more inclined to make in-game purchases and recommend the game to others, driving organic growth and revenue.

Developers can gather feedback through various channels, including in-game surveys, social media, forums, and direct communication. Each channel offers unique advantages and can reach different segments of the player base. For instance, in-game surveys provide immediate feedback from active players, while social media allows for broader community engagement.

Analyzing feedback requires a structured approach to identify common themes and actionable insights. Tools like sentiment analysis can help in categorizing feedback and prioritizing issues that need attention. Regularly updating the game based on feedback not only improves its quality but also keeps the community engaged and involved in the development process.

It is important to balance feedback with the overall vision and objectives of the game. While player suggestions are valuable, not all feedback should be implemented. Developers need to discern which changes will benefit the game and its monetisation strategy without compromising its core design and appeal.

Engaging with the player community through feedback also opens opportunities for beta testing new features and monetisation models. Players who participate in beta tests provide early insights and can help fine-tune aspects before a wider release, reducing the risk of negative reception.

Transparency in how feedback is used fosters a positive relationship between developers and players. Communicating the reasons behind certain decisions, especially when feedback is not implemented, helps manage expectations and maintain trust. Players appreciate when their contributions are acknowledged and can see their impact on the game.

Ultimately, player feedback is a valuable asset in developing a sustainable monetisation strategy. By continuously listening to and engaging with the player community, developers can create a game that not only meets player needs but also drives revenue growth. This dynamic interaction between players and developers is key to the success of mobile games in today's market.

15.2 Collecting and Analysing Feedback

Effective collection and analysis of player feedback are vital for refining game monetisation strategies. Various methods can be employed to gather feedback, each offering unique benefits and catering to different player segments.

In-game surveys are a direct way to collect feedback from active players. These surveys can be triggered at specific points in the game, such as after completing a level or making a purchase, to capture immediate reactions. Designing concise and targeted surveys ensures higher response rates and more relevant data. Questions should focus on player satisfaction, preferences, and suggestions for improvement.

Social media platforms provide a wealth of feedback from a broader audience. Players often share their experiences, suggestions, and grievances on platforms like Twitter, Facebook, and Reddit. Monitoring these channels allows developers to gauge public sentiment and identify trending issues. Social listening tools can automate this process, highlighting key topics and sentiment shifts.

Online forums and community boards are another valuable source of feedback. Dedicated game forums or platforms like Discord enable players to discuss the game in detail, share tips, and voice their opinions. Developers can participate in these discussions to gain deeper insights and foster a sense of community. Engaging with players in forums also helps in building trust and loyalty.

Direct communication, such as support tickets and emails, offers detailed and specific feedback from players. While this method might not provide a large volume of data, it often contains in-depth information about particular issues or suggestions. Personal responses to these communications can enhance player satisfaction and demonstrate a commitment to improvement.

Analyzing feedback involves categorizing and prioritizing the data collected. Sentiment analysis tools can be used to automatically categorize feedback into positive, negative, and neutral sentiments. This helps in identifying the overall player mood and pinpointing areas that need immediate attention. Additionally, feedback can be tagged based on themes, such as gameplay, graphics, or monetisation, to streamline the analysis process.

Identifying common themes and patterns in feedback is crucial for actionable insights. For example, recurring complaints about a specific feature or pricing model indicate a need for review and adjustment. On the other hand, positive feedback about certain aspects can highlight what is working well and should be maintained or expanded.

Once feedback is analyzed, it is important to prioritize the changes based on their potential impact on player satisfaction and monetisation. Not all feedback will be feasible or beneficial to implement, so developers need to evaluate the cost-benefit ratio of each suggestion. High-impact changes that align with the game's vision and monetisation goals should be prioritized.

Regularly revisiting and updating the analysis process ensures that the game continues to evolve with player expectations. As the player base grows and changes, so do their preferences and feedback. Keeping the feedback loop dynamic and responsive helps in maintaining player engagement and satisfaction over time.

Transparency in how feedback is handled is essential. Communicating with players about what feedback has been received, what actions will be taken, and the reasons behind those actions builds trust. This can be done through patch notes, developer blogs, or community updates. Acknowledging player contributions and explaining decisions fosters a positive relationship between developers and the community.

In conclusion, collecting and analyzing player feedback is a continuous process that plays a critical role in refining monetisation strategies. By effectively gathering, categorizing, and acting on feedback, developers can enhance the player experience, boost satisfaction, and ultimately drive revenue growth. This iterative process of feedback and improvement is key to the long-term success of mobile games.

15.3 Engaging with the Player Community

Engaging with the player community is crucial for fostering loyalty and improving monetisation in mobile games. A strong community creates a sense of belonging and investment among players, encouraging them to stay engaged and spend more on in-game purchases.

One effective way to engage with the player community is through regular communication. This can be achieved via social media updates, newsletters, and in-game announcements. Keeping players informed about upcoming features, events, and updates helps maintain their interest and excitement. Transparency about the development process and addressing player concerns openly builds trust and credibility.

Hosting events and contests is another excellent method to engage the community. In-game events, such as limited-time challenges or special rewards, incentivize players to log in and participate. Contests, both in-game and on social media, can generate excitement and encourage players to interact with each other and the developers. Rewards for participation and winning further enhance player engagement and satisfaction.

Creating and maintaining active forums and community boards is vital for fostering player interaction. Platforms like Discord, Reddit, and official game forums provide spaces where players can discuss the game, share tips, and offer feedback. Developers should actively participate in these forums to show they value player input and are part of the community.

User-generated content (UGC) is a powerful tool for community engagement. Encouraging players to create and share content, such as fan art, videos, and stories, fosters a deeper connection to the game. Featuring UGC on official channels and rewarding creators with in-game items or recognition motivates others to contribute, enhancing the community's vibrancy.

Regularly seeking player feedback through surveys, polls, and direct communication is essential for understanding their needs and preferences. Acknowledging feedback and implementing feasible suggestions shows players that their opinions matter, strengthening their loyalty. Providing updates on how feedback has influenced game development demonstrates a commitment to continuous improvement.

Building a team of community managers can significantly enhance engagement efforts. Community managers serve as the bridge between players and developers, addressing player concerns, moderating discussions, and facilitating events. Their presence ensures that the community remains active, positive, and aligned with the game's goals.

Offering exclusive content and early access to loyal community members can also boost engagement. Early access to new features or content creates a sense of privilege and rewards loyal players. Exclusive items or events for community members enhance their connection to the game and incentivize continued participation.

Regularly highlighting and celebrating player achievements and milestones can foster a sense of recognition and belonging. Publicly acknowledging top players, celebrating anniversaries, and showcasing impressive in-game accomplishments motivate players to stay engaged and strive for recognition.

Collaborating with influencers and content creators can extend the reach of community engagement efforts. Influencers have established audiences and can promote the game, events, and updates to a broader audience. Partnering with them for live streams, tutorials, and special events can attract new players and keep existing ones engaged.

Finally, maintaining a positive and inclusive community environment is essential for long-term engagement. Clear guidelines and active moderation ensure that discussions remain respectful and constructive. Encouraging positive behavior and swiftly addressing negative actions help create a welcoming atmosphere where all players feel valued and safe.

In summary, engaging with the player community is a multifaceted approach that involves regular communication, events, forums, UGC, feedback, community management, exclusive content, recognition, influencer collaborations, and a positive environment. By investing in these strategies, developers can foster a loyal and engaged community that supports the game's monetisation and growth.

15.4 Incorporating Feedback into Game Development

Incorporating player feedback into game development is essential for creating a game that resonates with its audience and drives monetisation. This process involves collecting feedback, analyzing it for actionable insights, and implementing changes that enhance the player experience.

The first step in incorporating feedback is to establish reliable channels for collection. In-game surveys, social media, forums, and direct communication are all valuable sources of feedback. It's important to make it easy for players to provide their opinions by integrating feedback options seamlessly into the game and its associated platforms.

Once feedback is collected, it needs to be analyzed systematically. Categorizing feedback based on themes such as gameplay mechanics, graphics, user interface, and monetisation helps in identifying common issues and areas for improvement. Sentiment analysis tools can be used to gauge overall player sentiment and prioritize feedback accordingly.

After analysis, the next step is to prioritize the feedback based on its potential impact on the player experience and monetisation. High-impact changes that align with the game's vision and goals should be prioritized. It's important to balance player desires with the feasibility and strategic direction of the game.

Implementing feedback requires a structured development process. Developers should create a roadmap that outlines which feedback will be addressed in upcoming updates and how it will be integrated into the game. Clear communication within the development team ensures that everyone is aligned on the changes and their expected outcomes.

Transparency with players about how their feedback is being used is crucial. Regular updates through patch notes, developer blogs, or community announcements keep players informed about upcoming changes and show that their input is valued. Highlighting specific feedback that has been implemented can enhance player satisfaction and trust.

Testing changes before a full release is vital to ensure they meet player expectations and function correctly. Beta testing with a subset of players can provide valuable insights and catch potential issues early. Feedback from beta testers can be used to fine-tune features before they are rolled out to the entire player base.

Iterating on feedback is an ongoing process. Even after implementing changes, it's important to continue collecting and analyzing feedback to ensure that the updates are well-received and effective. This iterative approach helps in continuously improving the game and maintaining player engagement.

Balancing feedback with the game's vision is essential. While player input is valuable, not all feedback will be feasible or beneficial to implement. Developers need to discern which changes will enhance the game and its monetisation strategy without compromising its core design and appeal.

Incorporating feedback also involves recognizing and addressing potential challenges. Sometimes, player suggestions might conflict with each other or with the game's overall strategy. Developers need to navigate these challenges thoughtfully, finding solutions that satisfy the majority of players while staying true to the game's objectives.

Finally, celebrating the positive impact of feedback can strengthen the relationship between players and developers. Showcasing success stories, such as improvements driven by player input, highlights the collaborative nature of the game's development and encourages continued engagement.

In conclusion, incorporating player feedback into game development is a dynamic and ongoing process that enhances the player experience and supports monetisation. By systematically collecting, analyzing, and implementing feedback, developers can create a game that resonates with its audience, fosters loyalty, and drives revenue growth. This collaborative approach between players and developers is key to the long-term success of mobile games.

15.5 Building Long-Term Player Loyalty

Building long-term player loyalty is essential for the sustained success and monetisation of mobile games. Loyal players are more likely to make repeated in-game purchases, participate in community events, and advocate for the game, driving organic growth.

One of the fundamental ways to build player loyalty is by delivering consistent and high-quality updates. Regularly introducing new content, features, and improvements keeps the game fresh and engaging. Players are more likely to remain invested in a game that evolves and offers new experiences over time.

Personalization is a powerful tool for fostering loyalty. Tailoring the game experience to individual players' preferences and behaviors can significantly enhance their connection to the game. Personalized offers, rewards, and content recommendations make players feel valued and understood.

Rewarding loyalty through in-game incentives is also effective. Implementing systems like daily login bonuses, loyalty programs, and exclusive rewards for long-term players encourages consistent engagement. These rewards can range from virtual goods to special access to events or features, providing tangible benefits for continued play.

Creating a strong narrative and emotional connection within the game can deepen player loyalty. Engaging storylines, memorable characters, and immersive worlds encourage players to become emotionally invested in the game. This connection makes players more likely to return and support the game financially.

Community building plays a crucial role in loyalty. Encouraging player interaction through social features, guilds, and multiplayer modes fosters a sense of belonging. Players who form friendships and social connections within the game are more likely to stay engaged and loyal.

Transparency and communication are key to maintaining player trust and loyalty. Keeping players informed about updates, addressing their concerns, and being open about development processes build credibility. Players appreciate honesty and are more likely to support a game that respects and values their input.

Listening to and acting on player feedback is critical. Players who see their suggestions and concerns addressed are more likely to feel a sense of ownership and loyalty towards the game. Regularly soliciting feedback and showing how it influences the game's development strengthens this bond.

Providing excellent customer support enhances player satisfaction and loyalty. Prompt and helpful responses to issues, along with clear and fair policies, make players feel respected and valued. A positive support experience can turn potentially negative situations into opportunities for building loyalty.

Exclusive content and early access for loyal players can also drive engagement. Offering beta access, special events, or unique items to long-term players makes them feel appreciated and privileged. This not only rewards loyalty but also incentivizes continued play.

Encouraging user-generated content (UGC) and recognizing player contributions can strengthen community ties. Highlighting fan art, player-created guides, and community events showcases the players' creativity and involvement. This recognition fosters a sense of pride and loyalty within the community.

Finally, evolving with player expectations and market trends is essential for long-term loyalty. Staying attuned to industry developments, player preferences, and technological advancements ensures that the game remains relevant and appealing. Adapting to these changes while maintaining the game's core values and vision keeps players engaged over time.

In summary, building long-term player loyalty involves delivering consistent updates, personalization, rewarding loyalty, creating strong narratives, fostering community, maintaining transparency, listening to feedback, providing excellent support, offering exclusive content, encouraging UGC, and evolving with market trends. By focusing on these strategies, developers can create a loyal player base that supports the game's sustained success and monetisation.

Chapter 16: Indie Developers and Monetisation

16.1 Monetisation Challenges for Indie Developers

Indie developers face unique challenges in monetising their mobile games. Limited resources, smaller teams, and less brand recognition can make it difficult to compete with larger studios. However, with the right strategies, indie developers can successfully monetise their games and build sustainable businesses.

One of the primary challenges for indie developers is funding. Developing a high-quality game requires investment in tools, assets, marketing, and more. Without sufficient funding, it can be challenging to bring a game to market and support post-launch activities. Indie developers often rely on personal savings, crowdfunding, or small investments, which can limit their financial flexibility.

Marketing is another significant challenge. Unlike major studios with large marketing budgets, indie developers must find cost-effective ways to promote their games. Building a strong online presence, leveraging social media, and engaging with gaming communities are essential but require time and effort. Effective marketing is crucial for visibility and attracting players in a crowded market.

Discoverability is closely linked to marketing challenges. With millions of games available on app stores, getting noticed is a major hurdle. Indie developers need to optimize their app store listings, use targeted keywords, and create compelling visuals and descriptions to stand out. Collaborating with influencers and securing media coverage can also boost discoverability.

Balancing monetisation with player experience is particularly critical for indie developers. Aggressive monetisation strategies can alienate players, especially if they perceive the game as pay-to-win. Indie developers need to design monetisation models that are fair and enhance the gameplay experience. This balance is essential for building a loyal player base and positive reputation.

Limited resources also impact the ability to implement and manage multiple monetisation strategies. Indie developers might need to choose between in-app purchases, ads, and premium models based on their capacity to develop and maintain these systems. Each monetisation method requires careful planning and execution to be effective.

Building and maintaining player engagement with limited resources is another challenge. Indie developers may struggle to release regular content updates or host events due to smaller teams. Engaging the community through social media, forums, and in-game events can help sustain player interest, but it requires ongoing effort.

Technical challenges, such as server management and security, can also be daunting. Ensuring a smooth and secure gaming experience is crucial for player retention and monetisation. Indie developers might need to invest in third-party services or hire experts to manage these aspects, adding to the financial burden.

Player feedback and support are vital but can be overwhelming for small teams. Responding to player queries, addressing issues, and incorporating feedback into updates require time and resources. Indie developers need to find efficient ways to manage player interactions while maintaining a positive relationship with their community.

Despite these challenges, indie developers have unique strengths that can aid in monetisation. Creativity, innovation, and a deep understanding of their player base allow indie developers to create unique and engaging games. These strengths can differentiate their games in the market and attract dedicated players.

Building a strong community around the game is a powerful asset. Indie developers can leverage their close connection with players to foster loyalty and advocacy. Engaged communities are more likely to support the game financially and spread the word, driving organic growth.

In conclusion, monetisation challenges for indie developers include funding, marketing, discoverability, balancing monetisation with player experience, limited resources, technical challenges, and player support. However, by leveraging their unique strengths and focusing on building strong communities, indie developers can overcome these challenges and successfully monetise their games.

16.2 Effective Strategies for Indies

Indie developers can employ several effective strategies to successfully monetise their mobile games. These strategies leverage the unique strengths of indie games and focus on building strong relationships with players.

One effective strategy is to adopt a hybrid monetisation model. Combining different monetisation methods, such as in-app purchases, ads, and premium features, can diversify revenue streams and reduce reliance on a single source. For example, offering a free-to-play game with optional in-app purchases and ad-supported gameplay can appeal to a broader audience.

Creating a compelling narrative and unique gameplay experience is crucial for indie games. Players are drawn to indie games for their creativity and innovation. By focusing on strong storytelling and distinctive mechanics, indie developers can attract dedicated players willing to support the game financially.

Leveraging social media and community engagement is vital for indie developers. Building an active presence on platforms like Twitter, Instagram, and TikTok allows developers to connect with players, share updates, and generate buzz. Engaging with gaming communities on Reddit, Discord, and other forums can also help in building a loyal player base.

Crowdfunding can be a valuable strategy for raising initial funds and building a community. Platforms like Kickstarter and Indiegogo allow developers to showcase their game, attract backers, and secure funding before launch. Successful crowdfunding campaigns not only provide financial support but also generate early interest and a dedicated fanbase.

Offering early access and beta testing to a select group of players can create a sense of exclusivity and investment. Early access players can provide valuable feedback, helping developers refine the game before a full release. This approach also builds anticipation and word-of-mouth promotion.

Utilizing influencer marketing can significantly boost visibility and attract new players. Collaborating with influencers who align with the game's target audience can introduce the game to a wider audience. Influencers can create gameplay videos, live streams, and reviews, generating interest and driving downloads.

Creating limited-time events and exclusive content can enhance player engagement and monetisation. Special events, seasonal updates, and exclusive in-game items encourage players to log in regularly and make purchases. These events create a sense of urgency and excitement, driving engagement and revenue.

Offering a premium version of the game with additional features or ad-free gameplay can appeal to players willing to pay for an enhanced experience. This approach provides a clear value proposition and caters to players who prefer a one-time purchase over ongoing spending.

Implementing a fair and transparent pricing strategy is essential for building trust and encouraging spending. Players are more likely to make in-app purchases if they perceive them as valuable and reasonably priced. Avoiding aggressive monetisation tactics ensures a positive player experience and long-term loyalty.

Focusing on user-generated content (UGC) can also drive engagement and monetisation. Encouraging players to create and share content, such as custom levels, skins, and mods, adds value to the game and fosters a sense of community. Recognizing and rewarding top creators can further motivate participation and enhance the game's appeal.

Regularly updating the game with new content, features, and improvements is crucial for retaining players and sustaining monetisation. Consistent updates keep the game fresh and exciting, encouraging players to stay engaged and make repeated purchases. Communicating these updates effectively through patch notes and social media builds anticipation and satisfaction.

In conclusion, effective monetisation strategies for indie developers include adopting hybrid models, creating compelling narratives, leveraging social media, crowdfunding, offering early access, influencer marketing, creating limited-time events, offering premium versions, implementing fair pricing, focusing on UGC, and regularly updating the game. By focusing on these strategies, indie developers can successfully monetise their games and build sustainable businesses.

16.3 Funding and Financial Planning

Funding and financial planning are critical aspects of indie game development. Securing adequate funding and managing finances effectively can make the difference between a successful launch and a stalled project.

Crowdfunding is a popular funding option for indie developers. Platforms like Kickstarter and Indiegogo allow developers to present their game concept to potential backers, raising funds before development is complete. A successful crowdfunding campaign not only provides financial support but also generates early interest and a dedicated community of supporters.

Grants and funding programs specifically for game development can also be valuable sources of funding. Various organizations, both governmental and private, offer grants to support indie developers. These grants often come with fewer strings attached than traditional investments, allowing developers to retain creative control.

Securing investment from venture capitalists or angel investors is another route, although it can be challenging. Investors typically look for projects with high growth potential and a solid business plan. Indie developers need to present a compelling case for their game's potential profitability and market appeal.

Revenue from early access and pre-orders can provide a financial boost before the full release. Offering early access versions of the game allows developers to generate revenue while continuing development. Pre-orders can also secure funds and gauge interest, helping with financial planning and marketing strategies.

Effective financial planning involves creating a detailed budget that accounts for all aspects of development, including tools, assets, marketing, and post-launch support. A well-structured budget helps in allocating resources efficiently and avoiding unexpected financial shortfalls.

Tracking expenses and revenue is crucial for maintaining financial health. Tools like accounting software can help developers monitor their finances, manage invoices, and prepare for taxes. Regular financial reviews ensure that the project stays on track and within budget.

Diversifying revenue streams can enhance financial stability. Relying on multiple monetisation methods, such as in-app purchases, ads, and premium versions, spreads financial risk. This approach ensures that the game generates income even if one revenue stream underperforms.

Managing cash flow is essential for sustaining development. Developers need to plan for periods of low income, especially during early development stages. Maintaining a financial buffer can help cover expenses during these times and prevent disruptions to the development process.

Understanding tax obligations and financial regulations is important for compliance and financial planning. Developers should familiarize themselves with the tax requirements in their region and consider consulting with a tax professional to ensure proper management of tax liabilities.

Collaborating with publishers can provide financial support and resources for marketing and distribution. While publishers take a share of the revenue, they can offer valuable assistance in reaching a wider audience and handling logistical aspects, allowing developers to focus on development.

Planning for post-launch support and updates is crucial for long-term success. Allocating funds for ongoing development, marketing, and community management ensures that the game remains engaging and profitable. Regular updates keep players invested and drive continued monetisation.

In conclusion, funding and financial planning are vital for the success of indie game development. Options such as crowdfunding, grants, investments, and early access can provide necessary funds, while effective financial planning ensures efficient resource allocation and financial stability. By managing finances wisely and diversifying revenue streams, indie developers can navigate the financial challenges of game development and build sustainable businesses.

16.4 Marketing and Monetisation for Indies

Marketing is a crucial component of monetisation for indie developers. Effective marketing strategies can significantly boost visibility, attract players, and drive revenue. Here are several key approaches that indie developers can use to market their games and enhance monetisation.

Building a strong online presence is essential. A well-designed website, active social media profiles, and engaging content help in creating a recognizable brand. Regular updates, behind-the-scenes content, and engaging with followers keep the community engaged and excited about the game.

Leveraging social media platforms is a cost-effective way to reach a broad audience. Platforms like Twitter, Instagram, TikTok, and Facebook allow developers to share updates, interact with players, and run promotional campaigns. Using hashtags, participating in trending topics, and collaborating with other developers can increase visibility.

Creating a compelling trailer and promotional materials is important for capturing interest. A well-crafted trailer that showcases the game's unique features, story, and gameplay can attract potential players and media attention. High-quality screenshots, concept art, and press kits also help in creating a professional image.

Influencer marketing can significantly boost visibility and credibility. Collaborating with influencers who align with the game's target audience can introduce the game to a wider player base. Influencers can create gameplay videos, live streams, and reviews, generating interest and driving downloads.

Participating in game expos, conventions, and online events provides opportunities to showcase the game to a broader audience. These events allow developers to network with industry professionals, gain media coverage, and receive valuable feedback from players. Virtual events and digital showcases have become increasingly popular and accessible.

Leveraging gaming communities and forums can help in building a dedicated player base. Engaging with communities on platforms like Reddit, Discord, and specialized gaming forums allows developers to connect with players, gather feedback, and promote their game. Hosting Q&A sessions, sharing development updates, and participating in discussions build community trust.

Press coverage and reviews play a significant role in marketing. Reaching out to gaming journalists, bloggers, and reviewers can result in articles, reviews, and features that enhance the game's credibility and visibility. A well-crafted press release and press kit make it easier for media outlets to cover the game.

Offering demos and beta access can generate early interest and feedback. Allowing players to experience a portion of the game before its full release creates anticipation and word-of-mouth promotion. Beta testing also provides valuable insights for refining the game and fixing potential issues.

Implementing email marketing campaigns can keep potential players informed and engaged. Collecting email addresses through the game's website or during events allows developers to send updates, exclusive offers, and launch announcements directly to interested players.

Running promotional campaigns and discounts can attract new players and boost sales. Time-limited discounts, special bundles, and holiday promotions create a sense of urgency and encourage purchases. Promoting these offers through social media and email marketing maximizes their reach.

Monitoring and analyzing marketing efforts is crucial for optimizing strategies. Using tools like Google Analytics, social media insights, and in-game analytics helps developers understand what works and what doesn't. This data-driven approach allows for continuous improvement and better targeting of marketing efforts.

In conclusion, effective marketing strategies are essential for monetising indie games. Building an online presence, leveraging social media, creating compelling promotional materials, collaborating with influencers, participating in events, engaging with communities, securing press coverage, offering demos, implementing email marketing, running promotions, and analyzing efforts are key approaches. By focusing on these strategies, indie developers can successfully market their games and drive revenue growth.

16.5 Success Stories of Indie Game Monetisation

Success stories of indie game monetisation provide valuable insights and inspiration for developers. These stories highlight the strategies and approaches that have led to significant financial success and player engagement. Here are some notable examples.

"Stardew Valley" by ConcernedApe is a prime example of indie game success. Developed by a single person, Eric Barone, the game has sold millions of copies worldwide. Barone focused on creating a rich, immersive experience with deep gameplay mechanics and a strong narrative. The game's success can be attributed to its engaging gameplay, frequent updates, and active community engagement. The decision to release on multiple platforms, including PC, consoles, and mobile, further boosted its reach and revenue.

"Undertale" by Toby Fox is another indie success story. The game garnered attention for its unique storytelling, humor, and innovative mechanics. Fox's use of a pay-what-you-want model for the game's soundtrack also contributed to its financial success. "Undertale" benefited from strong word-of-mouth promotion, positive reviews, and an active fan community. The game's success led to merchandise, spin-offs, and even a concert tour, diversifying its revenue streams.

"Hollow Knight" by Team Cherry showcases the impact of quality and community engagement. The game's hand-drawn art, challenging gameplay, and expansive world captivated players. Team Cherry successfully leveraged crowdfunding through Kickstarter to raise initial funds and build a dedicated community. Post-launch, they continued to engage with players through regular updates and expansions, maintaining interest and driving ongoing sales.

"Celeste" by Matt Makes Games achieved critical and commercial success through its compelling story and challenging platforming mechanics. The game's accessibility options and positive messages resonated with a wide audience. "Celeste" received numerous awards and accolades, further boosting its visibility and sales. The developer's transparency about the game's development and active community engagement also played a significant role in its success.

"Dead Cells" by Motion Twin exemplifies effective monetisation through early access. The game was initially released in early access, allowing players to experience and provide feedback during development. This approach helped in refining the game and building a dedicated player base. Upon full release, "Dead Cells" received widespread acclaim and commercial success, thanks to its polished gameplay and active community support.

"Cuphead" by Studio MDHR is renowned for its unique art style and challenging gameplay. The game's hand-drawn, 1930s cartoon-inspired visuals set it apart from other titles. Studio MDHR invested significant time and effort into perfecting the game's visuals and mechanics, resulting in critical acclaim and strong sales. The game's success led to merchandise, an animated series, and additional content, diversifying its revenue streams.

"Among Us" by InnerSloth highlights the impact of viral marketing and community engagement. Initially released with modest success, the game saw a surge in popularity through influencer and streamer coverage. The developers capitalized on this momentum by actively engaging with the community, adding new content, and improving the game based on player feedback. "Among Us" became a cultural phenomenon, driving massive downloads and revenue from in-app purchases.

"The Banner Saga" by Stoic Studio demonstrates the power of storytelling and art in indie game success. The game's visually striking art style and engaging narrative attracted a dedicated player base. Stoic Studio used Kickstarter to fund the game's development, building a community of backers who were invested in the game's success. The game's critical acclaim and positive word-of-mouth promotion led to strong sales and the development of sequels.

"Terraria" by Re-Logic showcases the long-term success of continuous updates and community engagement. Initially released in 2011, the game has remained popular due to regular updates, new content, and cross-platform availability. The developers' commitment to listening to player feedback and evolving the game has resulted in sustained success and a loyal player base.

These success stories highlight the importance of quality gameplay, strong community engagement, effective marketing, and innovative monetisation strategies. Indie developers can draw inspiration from these examples to create and monetize their own successful games.

In conclusion, success stories of indie game monetisation provide valuable lessons for developers. By focusing on quality, engaging with the community, leveraging marketing, and implementing innovative monetisation strategies, indie developers can achieve significant financial success and build sustainable businesses.

Chapter 17: Future of Mobile Game Monetisation

17.1 Predicting Market Trends

The mobile gaming industry is a dynamic landscape, characterized by rapid technological advancements and evolving player preferences. Predicting market trends is crucial for developers to stay competitive and relevant. One significant trend is the growing popularity of augmented reality (AR) and virtual reality (VR) games. These technologies offer immersive experiences that can be monetized through innovative strategies, such as AR-based in-game purchases and VR subscription models.

Another trend is the increasing use of artificial intelligence (AI) in game development and monetisation. AI can personalize player experiences by analyzing behavior patterns and tailoring in-game offers to individual preferences. This enhances player satisfaction and increases the likelihood of in-game purchases.

Blockchain technology is also gaining traction in the mobile gaming industry. It provides transparency and security, which can be leveraged for in-game transactions and the creation of unique, tradable digital assets. Blockchain-based games can implement decentralized economies, allowing players to own and trade virtual goods securely.

The rise of 5G technology will further influence mobile game monetisation. With faster and more reliable internet connections, developers can offer more complex and data-heavy games, enhancing the overall gaming experience. This can lead to new monetisation opportunities, such as cloud gaming subscriptions and real-time multiplayer experiences with in-game purchase options.

Social gaming is another trend that continues to grow. Games integrated with social media platforms encourage community building and peer influence, driving player engagement and spending. Developers can capitalize on this by creating socially interactive games with monetisation features like gifts, in-game currency, and special events.

Subscription models are becoming increasingly popular as they provide a steady revenue stream for developers. By offering exclusive content, early access, and ad-free experiences, subscription services can attract loyal players who are willing to pay a recurring fee.

The freemium model remains dominant, but there is a shift towards hybrid monetisation strategies. Combining free-to-play elements with premium features can cater to a broader audience and maximize revenue. Developers can experiment with various hybrid models, such as offering a free base game with optional paid expansions or integrating advertisements with in-app purchases.

Data-driven decision-making is essential for predicting market trends. Analyzing player data helps developers understand player behavior, preferences, and spending patterns. This information can be used to optimize game design, pricing strategies, and marketing campaigns, ensuring that monetisation efforts are effective and targeted.

Finally, ethical considerations are increasingly important in monetisation strategies. Players are becoming more aware of exploitative practices, and developers must prioritize fair and transparent monetisation methods. Implementing ethical monetisation practices can enhance player trust and loyalty, leading to long-term success.

In summary, predicting market trends involves staying informed about technological advancements, player preferences, and industry developments. By leveraging emerging technologies, adopting innovative monetisation models, and prioritizing ethical considerations, developers can navigate the future of mobile game monetisation successfully.

17.2 Potential Disruptors in the Industry

The mobile gaming industry is constantly evolving, with potential disruptors that could significantly impact monetisation strategies. One such disruptor is the rise of decentralized gaming platforms. These platforms leverage blockchain technology to create decentralized game economies where players have true ownership of in-game assets. This shift could undermine traditional monetisation methods, as players can trade assets outside the developer's ecosystem.

Another potential disruptor is the increasing regulatory scrutiny on loot boxes and similar monetisation mechanics. Governments and regulatory bodies worldwide are examining the ethical implications of these practices, which could lead to stricter regulations. Developers may need to adapt by finding alternative monetisation methods that comply with new laws and regulations.

The advancement of cloud gaming is also poised to disrupt the industry. Services like Google Stadia and NVIDIA GeForce Now allow players to stream games without needing high-end hardware. This shift could change how games are distributed and monetized, with subscription models and in-game purchases becoming more prominent in cloud-based ecosystems.

The emergence of the metaverse presents another potential disruption. As virtual worlds become more interconnected, the boundaries between different games and platforms may blur. Developers will need to consider how to monetize in a metaverse context, where players expect seamless transitions and interoperable assets across various games and platforms.

Artificial intelligence and machine learning are transforming game development and player interaction. AI-driven personalisation can enhance player experiences, but it also poses challenges for monetisation. Developers must balance AI-driven recommendations with ethical considerations to avoid manipulative practices.

Social media platforms are increasingly integrating gaming features, creating a new avenue for game distribution and monetisation. For example, platforms like Facebook and Instagram offer instant games and in-app purchases. This integration could disrupt traditional app stores and change how players discover and engage with mobile games.

The growing concern over data privacy and security is another potential disruptor. Players are becoming more cautious about sharing personal information, and developers must ensure robust data protection measures. Failure to do so can lead to loss of player trust and legal repercussions, impacting monetisation efforts.

The sustainability movement is also influencing the gaming industry. Players are becoming more environmentally conscious and prefer games developed with sustainable practices. Developers can leverage this trend by adopting eco-friendly development processes and promoting their commitment to sustainability as a unique selling point.

Augmented reality and virtual reality technologies continue to evolve, offering new ways to engage players. However, they also present challenges in terms of hardware requirements and user adoption. Developers must innovate to create compelling AR and VR experiences that justify the investment from players.

Lastly, the rise of indie games is disrupting traditional game development. Indie developers often adopt unique and innovative monetisation strategies, challenging established practices. Their success demonstrates that creativity and player-centric approaches can lead to profitable outcomes without relying on conventional monetisation methods.

In conclusion, the mobile gaming industry faces various potential disruptors, from technological advancements to regulatory changes and evolving player expectations. Developers must stay agile and adaptable, continuously exploring new monetisation opportunities while being mindful of emerging challenges and disruptions.

17.3 Evolving Player Expectations

As the mobile gaming industry matures, player expectations continue to evolve, influencing monetisation strategies. Modern players demand high-quality graphics, engaging narratives, and seamless gameplay experiences. Meeting these expectations requires significant investment in development, which must be balanced with effective monetisation.

Players today expect more value from in-game purchases. They seek items that enhance their gameplay experience rather than merely cosmetic upgrades. Developers must focus on creating meaningful in-game purchases that offer real value to players, such as power-ups, new levels, or exclusive content.

The rise of social gaming has led to increased expectations for community features. Players want to connect with friends, join clans, and participate in multiplayer events. Monetisation strategies can leverage these social interactions by offering exclusive social features, in-game currency for social activities, and community-driven content.

Personalisation is becoming a key expectation among players. They want games that adapt to their preferences and playstyles. Developers can use data analytics to personalize in-game offers and recommendations, enhancing player satisfaction and increasing the likelihood of purchases.

The trend towards ethical monetisation is also shaping player expectations. Players are becoming more aware of exploitative practices and prefer games that offer fair and transparent monetisation. Developers must prioritize ethical considerations, avoiding aggressive tactics like pay-to-win mechanics and focusing on player-centric monetisation models.

Subscription services are gaining popularity, with players appreciating the value of access to exclusive content and ad-free experiences. Developers can capitalize on this trend by offering subscription models that provide ongoing value, such as regular content updates, special events, and early access to new features.

Players are increasingly interested in cross-platform play, expecting their progress and purchases to be accessible across different devices. Developers must ensure seamless cross-platform integration to meet these expectations, allowing players to enjoy their games on multiple platforms without losing their progress or purchases.

Augmented reality (AR) and virtual reality (VR) are expanding player expectations for immersive experiences. Players want more than just traditional gameplay; they seek interactive and immersive environments. Developers can explore AR and VR monetisation opportunities, such as AR-based in-game purchases and VR-exclusive content.

The demand for high-quality, story-driven games is on the rise. Players expect rich narratives and engaging storytelling. Developers can monetize these experiences by offering episodic content, story expansions, and narrative-driven in-game purchases that enhance the overall story experience.

Players are becoming more health-conscious, expecting games to offer features that promote well-being. Developers can integrate health-focused features, such as reminders for breaks, fitness challenges, and mental wellness activities, potentially monetizing these features through premium subscriptions or in-app purchases.

Finally, the growing concern for data privacy means players expect robust data protection measures. Developers must prioritize data security and transparency, ensuring that players' personal information is safe. Building trust with players through strong privacy practices can enhance loyalty and long-term engagement.

In summary, evolving player expectations require developers to innovate and adapt their monetisation strategies. By focusing on quality, personalisation, ethical practices, and emerging technologies, developers can meet these expectations and create sustainable monetisation models.

17.4 Technological Advances and Monetisation

Technological advances are continually reshaping the mobile gaming industry, presenting new opportunities and challenges for monetisation. One of the most significant advancements is the widespread adoption of 5G technology. With its high-speed and low-latency capabilities, 5G enables more complex and data-intensive games, offering new avenues for monetisation through enhanced gameplay experiences and real-time multiplayer features.

Augmented reality (AR) and virtual reality (VR) technologies are also transforming mobile gaming. AR games overlay digital content onto the real world, creating immersive experiences that can be monetized through in-game purchases and location-based advertising. VR games provide fully immersive environments, allowing for unique monetisation strategies such as VR-exclusive content and subscription models.

Artificial intelligence (AI) and machine learning are revolutionizing game development and player engagement. AI can analyze player behavior to offer personalized in-game purchases, recommend content, and adjust difficulty levels to keep players engaged. Machine learning algorithms can predict player churn and identify high-value players, enabling targeted monetisation efforts.

Blockchain technology is introducing new possibilities for secure and transparent in-game transactions. Blockchain-based games can offer decentralized economies where players truly own their digital assets. These assets can be traded or sold outside the game, creating new monetisation opportunities through transaction fees and unique digital goods.

The advancement of cloud gaming platforms is another technological shift impacting monetisation. Cloud gaming allows players to stream games on any device without needing high-end hardware. This technology supports subscription-based models, where players pay a monthly fee to access a library of games, and in-game purchases can be seamlessly integrated across devices.

Big data and analytics are becoming essential tools for developers to optimize monetisation strategies. By collecting and analyzing player data, developers can gain insights into player preferences, spending habits, and engagement patterns. This information can inform pricing strategies, content updates, and personalized offers, enhancing overall monetisation effectiveness.

Voice recognition technology is also making its way into mobile games. Voice commands can create more interactive and immersive experiences, opening new monetisation opportunities such as voice-activated purchases and in-game advertisements. Additionally, integrating voice assistants can enhance player support and engagement.

Wearable technology is expanding the boundaries of mobile gaming. Devices like smartwatches and fitness trackers can be integrated with mobile games to offer unique gameplay experiences and monetisation opportunities. For example, developers can create fitness-based games that encourage physical activity and monetize through in-app purchases for fitness gear or premium features.

The rise of the Internet of Things (IoT) is enabling more interconnected gaming experiences. IoT devices can enhance gameplay by providing real-world data that influences in-game events. This interconnectivity can be monetized through partnerships with brands and in-game advertising based on real-time data.

Finally, advances in graphics and processing power are allowing for more visually stunning and complex games. High-quality graphics and realistic animations can attract players and justify premium pricing for in-game content and purchases. Developers can leverage these technological advancements to create visually appealing games that offer a wide range of monetisation options.

In conclusion, technological advances are driving innovation in mobile game monetisation. By embracing these technologies, developers can create engaging and immersive experiences that offer new and diverse monetisation opportunities.

17.5 Long-Term Sustainability of Current Models

The long-term sustainability of current mobile game monetisation models is a topic of significant importance. As the industry evolves, developers must ensure that their monetisation strategies remain viable and profitable. One key factor in achieving sustainability is diversifying revenue streams. Relying solely on one monetisation method, such as in-app purchases or advertisements, can be risky. Developers should explore multiple revenue streams, including subscriptions, sponsorships, and merchandise.

Player retention is crucial for sustainable monetisation. Keeping players engaged over the long term ensures a steady stream of revenue. Developers can implement retention strategies such as regular content updates, community events, and loyalty programs. By continuously offering new content and incentives, developers can maintain player interest and spending.

Transparency and fairness in monetisation practices are essential for building long-term player trust. Players are becoming more aware of exploitative monetisation tactics, and negative perceptions can lead to decreased engagement and revenue. Developers should prioritize ethical monetisation practices, clearly communicating the value of in-game purchases and avoiding pay-to-win mechanics.

The freemium model, while popular, faces sustainability challenges due to market saturation and player fatigue. Developers can address these challenges by innovating within the freemium framework, offering unique value propositions and enhancing the overall player experience. Hybrid models that combine free-to-play elements with premium content can also provide a balanced approach.

Adapting to changing regulations is another critical aspect of sustainability. As governments impose stricter regulations on loot boxes and in-game purchases, developers must comply with new laws and adjust their monetisation strategies accordingly. Staying informed about regulatory changes and proactively implementing compliant practices can prevent legal issues and maintain player trust.

The rise of subscription services presents a sustainable monetisation model. Subscriptions provide a consistent revenue stream and foster player loyalty by offering exclusive content and benefits. Developers can create tiered subscription models to cater to different player segments, ensuring accessibility while maximizing revenue potential.

Data-driven decision-making enhances sustainability by optimizing monetisation strategies. Analyzing player data helps developers understand spending patterns, preferences, and engagement levels. This information can inform pricing strategies, content updates, and targeted offers, ensuring that monetisation efforts are effective and aligned with player expectations.

Cross-platform play is becoming increasingly important for sustainability. Allowing players to access their games across multiple devices ensures continuous engagement and spending. Developers should focus on creating seamless cross-platform experiences, where players can carry their progress and purchases across different devices.

Community engagement is vital for long-term sustainability. Building a strong player community fosters loyalty and word-of-mouth promotion. Developers can engage with their community through social media, forums, and in-game events. Encouraging player feedback and incorporating it into game development shows players that their opinions are valued, enhancing their overall experience.

Finally, innovation is key to sustaining monetisation models. The mobile gaming industry is highly competitive, and developers must continuously innovate to stay ahead. This includes exploring new technologies, experimenting with different monetisation strategies, and staying attuned to player preferences. By fostering a culture of innovation, developers can adapt to changing market conditions and maintain sustainable monetisation practices.

In conclusion, the long-term sustainability of mobile game monetisation models depends on diversification, player retention, ethical practices, regulatory compliance, data-driven decisions, cross-platform play, community engagement, and continuous innovation. By addressing these factors, developers can create sustainable and profitable monetisation strategies.

Chapter 18: Tools and Resources for Developers

18.1 Monetisation Platforms and Tools

In the ever-evolving landscape of mobile game development, leveraging the right monetisation platforms and tools is crucial for success. These tools help developers implement, manage, and optimize their monetisation strategies effectively. One of the most widely used platforms is Unity Ads, which offers robust tools for integrating ads seamlessly into games. Unity Ads provides various ad formats, including rewarded videos and interstitial ads, allowing developers to choose the best fit for their game's experience.

AdMob by Google is another popular monetisation platform. It offers a comprehensive suite of tools for displaying ads, including banner ads, interstitial ads, and native ads. AdMob's advanced analytics help developers understand ad performance and optimize their monetisation strategies accordingly. The platform's mediation feature also enables developers to maximize revenue by integrating multiple ad networks.

IronSource is renowned for its user-friendly interface and powerful monetisation capabilities. It provides tools for implementing rewarded videos, offerwalls, and interstitial ads. IronSource's mediation feature ensures that developers can achieve high fill rates and eCPMs by utilizing multiple ad networks. Additionally, the platform offers robust analytics and reporting tools to track and optimize monetisation performance.

For in-app purchases, Apple's StoreKit and Google Play Billing are essential tools. These platforms allow developers to integrate in-app purchase functionalities, manage subscriptions, and handle payment processing. They also provide APIs for implementing features like promo codes, purchase validation, and user authentication.

Fyber is another versatile monetisation platform that supports a wide range of ad formats, including rewarded videos, interstitials, and banners. Fyber's FairBid mediation tool optimizes ad revenue by dynamically allocating traffic to the highest-performing ad networks. The platform also offers comprehensive analytics and reporting features to monitor and enhance monetisation performance.

Chartboost is a leading platform for mobile game advertising and monetisation. It offers tools for implementing interstitial ads, rewarded videos, and in-play ads. Chartboost's Direct Deals Marketplace allows developers to negotiate directly with advertisers, potentially increasing ad revenue. The platform also provides in-depth analytics and user segmentation features to refine monetisation strategies.

MoPub, acquired by Twitter, is a robust ad serving platform that supports various ad formats, including banners, interstitials, and native ads. MoPub's Advanced Bidding feature helps developers maximize ad revenue by enabling real-time bidding from multiple demand sources. The platform's analytics tools provide insights into ad performance and user engagement, facilitating data-driven monetisation decisions.

In addition to these platforms, developers can benefit from analytics tools like Firebase Analytics and GameAnalytics. Firebase Analytics offers comprehensive insights into user behavior, in-app purchases, and ad performance. It integrates seamlessly with other Firebase services, providing a holistic view of app performance and user engagement. GameAnalytics specializes in game-specific metrics, offering detailed reports on player behavior, retention, and monetisation.

For optimizing in-game economies and pricing strategies, developers can use tools like SOOMLA and adjust. SOOMLA provides analytics on in-game purchases and virtual economy health, helping developers identify trends and optimize pricing. Adjust offers advanced attribution and analytics tools to track user acquisition, measure campaign performance, and optimize monetisation efforts.

Finally, social media platforms like Facebook and Instagram offer tools for promoting games and driving user engagement. Facebook Audience Network enables developers to monetize their games with targeted ads, while Instagram provides opportunities for influencer marketing and community building.

In conclusion, a wide range of monetisation platforms and tools are available to mobile game developers. By leveraging these tools, developers can implement effective monetisation strategies, optimize ad performance, and maximize revenue.

18.2 Analytics and Data Management Tools

Analytics and data management tools are essential for mobile game developers to understand player behavior, optimize gameplay experiences, and enhance monetisation strategies. Firebase Analytics, one of the most popular tools, offers comprehensive insights into user engagement, retention, and in-app purchases. Its integration with other Firebase services, such as Firebase Remote Config and Firebase Cloud Messaging, allows developers to create personalized experiences and targeted marketing campaigns.

GameAnalytics is another powerful tool designed specifically for game developers. It provides detailed reports on player behavior, including session length, progression, and in-game events. The platform also offers customizable dashboards and benchmarking features, enabling developers to compare their game's performance against industry standards and identify areas for improvement.

Adjust is renowned for its advanced attribution and analytics capabilities. It helps developers track user acquisition sources, measure the effectiveness of marketing campaigns, and analyze user behavior across different channels. Adjust's fraud prevention features ensure the integrity of data, protecting developers from fraudulent activities that could skew their analytics.

Mixpanel is a versatile analytics tool that offers deep insights into user behavior and engagement. Its event-based tracking system allows developers to monitor specific actions within the game, such as level completions, in-app purchases, and social interactions. Mixpanel's A/B testing feature enables developers to experiment with different game elements and determine the most effective strategies for player retention and monetisation.

Amplitude is another robust analytics platform that focuses on user behavior and product intelligence. It provides real-time analytics, cohort analysis, and user segmentation features, allowing developers to understand how players interact with their game over time. Amplitude's Behavioral Cohorts feature helps identify patterns in user behavior, enabling developers to tailor their monetisation strategies to different player segments.

Heap Analytics offers an automated approach to data collection and analysis. It captures all user interactions within the game without requiring manual event tagging. This comprehensive data collection allows developers to analyze player behavior, identify trends, and make data-driven decisions to enhance gameplay and monetisation.

For data visualization and reporting, Tableau is a powerful tool that helps developers create interactive dashboards and visualizations. Tableau's drag-and-drop interface makes it easy to analyze complex data sets and share insights with stakeholders. Its integration capabilities with various data sources ensure that developers can access and analyze all relevant data in one place.

BigQuery, a fully-managed data warehouse by Google, enables developers to perform fast SQL queries on large datasets. Its scalability and integration with other Google Cloud services make it an ideal choice for developers handling vast amounts of game data. BigQuery's machine learning capabilities also allow developers to build predictive models and gain deeper insights into player behavior.

Kochava is a comprehensive analytics and attribution platform that provides insights into user acquisition, engagement, and monetisation. It offers advanced features like cohort analysis, user journey mapping, and real-time data visualization. Kochava's integration with various ad networks and marketing platforms ensures that developers can track the effectiveness of their campaigns and optimize their monetisation strategies.

Finally, DeltaDNA offers specialized analytics tools for game developers, focusing on player behavior and in-game economy. It provides features like real-time analytics, player segmentation, and predictive modeling. DeltaDNA's CRM tools enable developers to create personalized marketing campaigns and improve player retention through targeted messaging and rewards.

In conclusion, analytics and data management tools are critical for mobile game developers to understand player behavior, optimize gameplay, and enhance monetisation. By leveraging these tools, developers can make data-driven decisions, improve player engagement, and maximize revenue.

18.3 Best Practices and Guidelines

Implementing effective monetisation strategies in mobile games requires adherence to best practices and guidelines to ensure success and maintain player satisfaction. One of the fundamental best practices is to prioritize player experience. Monetisation strategies should be integrated seamlessly into the game without disrupting gameplay. Players should feel that in-game purchases and ads enhance their experience rather than hinder it.

Transparency in monetisation is crucial. Developers should clearly communicate the value of in-game purchases and avoid misleading players. Pricing should be transparent, and players should understand what they are getting for their money. This builds trust and encourages players to spend more willingly.

Balancing the in-game economy is another important practice. Developers should ensure that virtual goods and in-game currency are priced appropriately, providing value to players without creating a pay-to-win environment. Regularly reviewing and adjusting prices based on player feedback and data analysis helps maintain a balanced economy.

Offering a variety of monetisation options caters to different player preferences. Some players prefer one-time purchases, while others might opt for subscriptions or ads. By providing multiple monetisation methods, developers can appeal to a broader audience and maximize revenue potential.

Rewarding players for engagement is a powerful monetisation strategy. Implementing reward systems, such as daily login bonuses, achievement rewards, and loyalty programs, encourages players to stay engaged and spend more time in the game. These rewards can be tied to in-game purchases, providing additional incentives for players to spend money.

Ethical considerations in monetisation are increasingly important. Developers should avoid exploitative practices, such as excessive use of loot boxes or aggressive pay-to-win mechanics. Prioritizing fair and ethical monetisation practices not only enhances player satisfaction but also builds a positive reputation for the game and the developer.

Personalisation of monetisation offers can significantly increase their effectiveness. Using data analytics, developers can tailor in-game offers and ads to individual player preferences and behaviors. Personalized offers are more likely to resonate with players and lead to higher conversion rates.

Regularly updating content is essential for maintaining player interest and driving monetisation. Providing fresh content, such as new levels, characters, and events, keeps the game exciting and encourages players to make purchases. Announcing upcoming updates and creating anticipation can also boost player engagement and spending.

Testing and iterating monetisation strategies is a best practice that cannot be overlooked. A/B testing different monetisation approaches, such as varying the prices of virtual goods or testing different ad placements, helps identify the most effective strategies. Continuous iteration based on player feedback and data analysis ensures that monetisation methods remain effective and aligned with player preferences.

Ensuring a seamless payment process is crucial for maximizing in-game purchases. The checkout process should be quick, easy, and secure. Implementing multiple payment options, such as credit cards, digital wallets, and carrier billing, accommodates different player preferences and increases the likelihood of successful transactions.

Finally, engaging with the player community is vital for long-term success. Developers should actively seek and incorporate player feedback into their monetisation strategies. Engaging with the community through social media, forums, and in-game events builds a loyal player base and fosters a positive relationship between players and developers.

In conclusion, adhering to best practices and guidelines in monetisation ensures that mobile games provide a satisfying player experience while maximizing revenue. By prioritizing player experience, transparency, ethical considerations, and continuous improvement, developers can implement effective and sustainable monetisation strategies.

18.4 Resources for Continuous Learning

The mobile gaming industry is constantly evolving, and developers must engage in continuous learning to stay ahead of trends and innovations. Numerous resources are available to help developers expand their knowledge and skills in game monetisation.

Online courses and tutorials are valuable resources for developers at all levels. Platforms like Udemy, Coursera, and LinkedIn Learning offer courses on game development, monetisation strategies, and data analytics. These courses often include practical examples and case studies, providing developers with actionable insights and techniques.

Industry conferences and events are excellent opportunities for networking and learning. Events such as the Game Developers Conference (GDC), Casual Connect, and Pocket Gamer Connects feature sessions on the latest trends in game development and monetisation. Attending these conferences allows developers to learn from industry experts, discover new tools and technologies, and connect with peers.

Professional organizations and associations, such as the International Game Developers Association (IGDA), provide valuable resources for continuous learning. Membership often includes access to webinars, workshops, industry reports, and networking opportunities. Engaging with these organizations helps developers stay informed about industry developments and best practices.

Developer forums and communities are essential for sharing knowledge and experiences. Platforms like Reddit, Stack Overflow, and specialized game development forums offer spaces for developers to ask questions, share insights, and discuss monetisation strategies. Participating in these communities fosters collaborative learning and problem-solving.

Books and publications are valuable resources for in-depth knowledge. Books like "Free-to-Play: Making Money from Games You Give Away" by Will Luton and "The Art of Game Design: A Book of Lenses" by Jesse Schell provide comprehensive insights into game design and monetisation. Industry publications such as Gamasutra and Game Developer Magazine offer articles, interviews, and case studies on the latest trends and best practices.

Podcasts and webinars are convenient resources for continuous learning. Podcasts like "The GameDev.tv Podcast" and "GameDev Loadout" feature interviews with industry professionals and discussions on game development and monetisation. Webinars hosted by game development platforms, industry organizations, and educational institutions provide deep dives into specific topics and interactive learning experiences.

Mentorship programs can significantly enhance learning and professional development. Organizations like IGDA and local game developer associations often offer mentorship programs connecting experienced developers with newcomers. Mentors provide guidance, feedback, and insights based on their experiences, helping mentees navigate challenges and grow their skills.

Online communities and social media groups focused on game development and monetisation are valuable for staying updated and engaging with peers. LinkedIn groups, Facebook communities, and Discord servers offer platforms for discussing trends, sharing resources, and seeking advice. Engaging with these communities helps developers build relationships and stay informed.

Open-source projects and collaborative initiatives provide hands-on learning opportunities. Participating in open-source game development projects allows developers to gain practical experience, collaborate with others, and contribute to the community. Platforms like GitHub host numerous open-source projects where developers can contribute and learn from others' code.

Finally, staying informed about industry trends and news is crucial for continuous learning. Subscribing to newsletters, blogs, and industry reports from sources like Sensor Tower, App Annie, and Newzoo provides regular updates on market trends, player behavior, and monetisation strategies. Keeping up with the latest news ensures that developers are aware of emerging opportunities and challenges.

In conclusion, continuous learning is essential for mobile game developers to stay competitive and innovative. By leveraging online courses, industry events, professional organizations, communities, publications, podcasts, mentorship programs, open-source projects, and industry news, developers can expand their knowledge and skills in game monetisation.

18.5 Community and Networking Opportunities

Building a strong community and leveraging networking opportunities are crucial for the success and growth of mobile game developers. Engaging with the player community and industry peers fosters collaboration, innovation, and support, leading to better game development and monetisation outcomes.

Developer conferences and events provide excellent networking opportunities. Events like the Game Developers Conference (GDC), E3, and IndieCade bring together industry professionals from around the world. Attending these conferences allows developers to connect with peers, share experiences, and learn about the latest trends and technologies. Networking at these events can lead to valuable partnerships, mentorship opportunities, and collaborations.

Online forums and communities are essential for continuous engagement and knowledge sharing. Platforms like Reddit, Stack Overflow, and specialized game development forums offer spaces for developers to ask questions, share insights, and discuss challenges. Participating in these communities helps developers build relationships, gain feedback, and stay updated on industry developments.

Social media platforms like Twitter, LinkedIn, and Facebook provide opportunities for networking and community building. Following industry leaders, joining game development groups, and participating in discussions can help developers stay informed and connected. Engaging with social media communities also allows developers to promote their games, gather player feedback, and build a following.

Local game developer meetups and associations offer opportunities for in-person networking and collaboration. Organizations like the International Game Developers Association (IGDA) have local chapters that host regular events, workshops, and networking sessions. Participating in local meetups helps developers connect with peers in their region, share resources, and collaborate on projects.

Game jams and hackathons are valuable for community building and skill development. Events like Global Game Jam, Ludum Dare, and local hackathons provide opportunities for developers to work together on short-term projects, experiment with new ideas, and learn from each other. Participating in game jams fosters creativity, teamwork, and innovation.

Online communities and Discord servers focused on game development offer real-time interaction and collaboration. Platforms like Discord host numerous game development servers where developers can chat, share resources, and seek advice. Joining these communities provides continuous support and engagement with peers.

Collaborative projects and open-source initiatives provide opportunities for hands-on learning and networking. Contributing to open-source game development projects on platforms like GitHub allows developers to collaborate with others, learn from their code, and build a portfolio of work. Collaborative projects foster a sense of community and shared purpose.

Mentorship programs and initiatives are valuable for professional growth and networking. Organizations like IGDA offer mentorship programs that connect experienced developers with newcomers. Mentors provide guidance, feedback, and support, helping mentees navigate challenges and grow their skills. Building relationships with mentors and peers through these programs enhances professional development.

Participating in online courses and webinars also offers networking opportunities. Platforms like Udemy, Coursera, and LinkedIn Learning host interactive courses and webinars where developers can engage with instructors and peers. Asking questions, participating in discussions, and connecting with other learners can lead to valuable networking and collaboration.

Finally, engaging with the player community is crucial for building a loyal following and gathering feedback. Developers can use social media, forums, and in-game events to interact with players, gather feedback, and build relationships. Creating a positive and responsive community enhances player loyalty and supports long-term success.

In conclusion, building a strong community and leveraging networking opportunities are essential for mobile game developers. By participating in conferences, online forums, social media, local meetups, game jams, collaborative projects, mentorship programs, online courses, and player interactions, developers can foster collaboration, innovation, and support, leading to better game development and monetisation outcomes.

Chapter 19: Building a Monetisation Strategy

19.1 Steps to Develop a Monetisation Plan

Developing a monetisation plan is crucial for the success of a mobile game. The following steps outline a structured approach to creating an effective monetisation strategy:

1. **Market Research**: Conduct thorough market research to understand current trends, player preferences, and competitive landscape. Analyze successful games in your genre and identify the monetisation strategies they use.
2. **Define Objectives**: Clearly define your monetisation objectives. These could include revenue targets, player retention goals, or enhancing user engagement. Having specific, measurable objectives will guide your strategy.
3. **Identify Target Audience**: Understand who your players are. Develop detailed player personas that include demographic information, gaming habits, spending behavior, and preferences. This will help tailor your monetisation approach to meet their needs.
4. **Choose Monetisation Models**: Select the monetisation models that align with your game and audience. Options include free-to-play (F2P), premium, freemium, subscription, and hybrid models. Each has its pros and cons, so choose wisely based on your game design and player base.
5. **Design In-Game Economy**: Create a balanced in-game economy that supports your monetisation strategy. This includes setting prices for virtual goods, designing in-game currency systems, and ensuring that there is value in spending money within the game.
6. **Implement In-Game Purchases**: Integrate in-game purchase options seamlessly into the gameplay. Ensure that the process is user-friendly and that purchases offer real value to players. Consider offering both consumable and non-consumable items.
7. **Integrate Advertising**: If using in-game ads, choose formats that do not disrupt gameplay. Options include rewarded videos, interstitials, and banner ads. Balance the frequency and placement of ads to avoid frustrating players.
8. **Develop Retention Strategies**: Focus on player retention to support long-term monetisation. Implement features like daily rewards, special events, and social interactions to keep players engaged and coming back to the game.
9. **Test and Optimize**: Continuously test different aspects of your monetisation strategy. Use A/B testing to determine what works best and make data-driven adjustments. Monitor key metrics such as conversion rates, average revenue per user (ARPU), and player feedback.
10. **Launch and Monitor**: Launch your game with the monetisation strategies in place. Closely monitor performance and be prepared to make quick adjustments based on player behavior and feedback.

160 | THEORY AND IMPLEMENTATION DEVELOPMENT

By following these steps, developers can create a robust monetisation plan that maximizes revenue while ensuring a positive player experience.

19.2 Identifying Target Audience and Goals

Identifying the target audience and setting clear goals are fundamental steps in developing a successful monetisation strategy. Here's how to approach these tasks:

1. **Segmentation Analysis**: Start by segmenting the potential player base. Use criteria such as age, gender, geographic location, and gaming preferences. This helps in creating specific marketing and monetisation strategies tailored to each segment.
2. **Player Personas**: Develop detailed player personas that represent the different segments of your audience. These personas should include information about their gaming habits, spending behavior, and preferences. For example, a persona might be a 25-year-old male who enjoys strategy games and spends moderately on in-game purchases.
3. **Surveys and Feedback**: Conduct surveys and gather feedback from potential players. This direct input can provide insights into what players want and are willing to pay for. Use this information to refine your monetisation strategies.
4. **Competitor Analysis**: Analyze competitors' games and their target audiences. Identify what works for them and what doesn't. This can provide valuable insights and help you position your game effectively in the market.
5. **Setting Goals**: Define clear, measurable goals for your monetisation strategy. Goals could include achieving a certain ARPU, reaching a specific number of active users, or maintaining a high retention rate. Ensure that these goals are aligned with your overall business objectives.
6. **Behavioral Insights**: Use data analytics to understand player behavior within your game. Track metrics such as session length, frequency of play, and purchase patterns. This data can help in identifying high-value players and tailoring offers to them.
7. **Personalization**: Leverage the information about your target audience to create personalized experiences. This can include tailored in-game offers, personalized messages, and dynamic pricing strategies that adjust based on player behavior.
8. **Community Engagement**: Engage with your player community through social media, forums, and in-game events. Building a strong community can provide ongoing feedback and help in fine-tuning your monetisation strategies.
9. **Market Adaptation**: Be prepared to adapt your strategy based on market trends and player preferences. The gaming industry is dynamic, and staying flexible can help you stay ahead of the competition.
10. **Tracking Progress**: Regularly track the progress towards your goals using key performance indicators (KPIs). These might include daily active users (DAU), monthly active users (MAU), retention rates, and revenue metrics. Adjust your strategies as needed based on these metrics.

Identifying the target audience and setting clear goals are critical for the success of any monetisation strategy. By understanding who your players are and what they want, you can create tailored experiences that drive engagement and revenue.

19.3 Creating a Sustainable Monetisation Model

Creating a sustainable monetisation model involves designing systems that generate consistent revenue while maintaining a positive player experience. Here's how to approach this task:

1. **Long-Term Vision**: Develop a long-term vision for your game's monetisation. Consider how the game will evolve over time and how monetisation strategies will adapt to keep players engaged and spending.
2. **Player Value Proposition**: Clearly define the value proposition for players. What do they get in return for their spending? Ensure that in-game purchases enhance the gameplay experience and offer real value.
3. **Balancing Free and Paid Content**: Strike a balance between free and paid content. Free players should still enjoy the game, while paying players receive additional benefits that enhance their experience. Avoid pay-to-win mechanics that can alienate non-paying players.
4. **In-Game Economy Design**: Design a robust in-game economy that supports your monetisation model. This includes setting prices for virtual goods, managing currency flow, and ensuring that there are meaningful ways for players to spend money.
5. **Diverse Revenue Streams**: Diversify your revenue streams to reduce reliance on a single source. This can include in-game purchases, subscriptions, advertising, and partnerships. A diverse revenue model can provide more stability.
6. **Engagement and Retention**: Focus on player engagement and retention. Use features like daily rewards, special events, and social interactions to keep players coming back. High retention rates lead to more opportunities for monetisation.
7. **Ethical Monetisation**: Ensure that your monetisation practices are ethical. Avoid exploiting players or using manipulative tactics. Transparent pricing and fair value for money are essential for building trust with your player base.
8. **Data-Driven Decisions**: Use data analytics to inform your monetisation strategies. Track player behaviour, spending patterns, and feedback to make informed decisions. Regularly update your strategies based on data insights.
9. **Iterative Testing**: Continuously test and iterate your monetisation strategies. Use A/B testing to experiment with different approaches and identify what works best. Be prepared to make adjustments based on player feedback and performance metrics.
10. **Community Building**: Invest in community building. Engage with your players through social media, forums, and in-game events. A strong community can provide valuable feedback and foster loyalty, leading to sustained revenue.
11. **Adaptation to Trends**: Stay adaptable to market trends and technological advancements. The gaming industry is rapidly evolving, and staying ahead of trends can give you a competitive edge.
12. **Scalability**: Design your monetisation model to be scalable. As your player base grows, your monetisation strategies should be able to scale with it. This includes ensuring that your infrastructure can handle increased traffic and transactions.
13. **Legal and Compliance**: Ensure that your monetisation practices comply with legal and regulatory requirements. This includes consumer protection laws, data privacy regulations, and industry standards.

14. **Feedback Loop**: Establish a feedback loop with your players. Regularly collect and analyze feedback to understand their needs and preferences. Use this information to refine your monetisation strategies.
15. **Transparency**: Be transparent with your players about how monetisation works in your game. Clear communication about pricing, value, and benefits helps build trust and encourages spending.

Creating a sustainable monetisation model is a continuous process that requires a deep understanding of your players, market trends, and data insights. By focusing on long-term value and ethical practices, developers can create monetisation strategies that support both revenue growth and player satisfaction.

19.4 Implementing and Testing Strategies

Implementing and testing monetisation strategies is a critical phase in ensuring their effectiveness and sustainability. Here's how to approach this process:

1. **Prototype Development**: Start by developing prototypes of your monetisation strategies. This can include mock-ups of in-game stores, ad placements, and virtual goods. Use these prototypes to gather initial feedback from a small group of players.
2. **A/B Testing**: Implement A/B testing to compare different monetisation strategies. For example, test different price points for virtual goods or various ad formats. Analyze which version performs better in terms of revenue and player satisfaction.
3. **Gradual Rollout**: Consider a gradual rollout of monetisation features. Introduce new elements to a small segment of your player base first. This allows you to test their impact and make adjustments before a full-scale launch.
4. **Player Feedback**: Collect and analyze player feedback during the testing phase. Use surveys, focus groups, and in-game feedback mechanisms to understand player reactions and preferences. Adjust your strategies based on this feedback.
5. **Data Analytics**: Leverage data analytics to monitor the performance of your monetisation strategies. Track key metrics such as conversion rates, ARPU, retention rates, and player engagement. Use this data to identify trends and areas for improvement.
6. **Iterative Refinement**: Based on the feedback and data collected, iteratively refine your monetisation strategies. Make incremental changes and continuously test their impact. This iterative approach helps in optimizing strategies for better performance.
7. **User Experience (UX) Testing**: Conduct UX testing to ensure that monetisation elements are seamlessly integrated into the game. The purchasing process should be intuitive and frictionless. Avoid intrusive ads or complicated purchase flows that can frustrate players.
8. **Revenue Forecasting**: Use the data from your tests to forecast potential revenue. This helps in setting realistic financial goals and understanding the long-term viability of your monetisation strategies.
9. **Compliance Check**: Ensure that your monetisation strategies comply with all relevant legal and regulatory requirements. This includes consumer protection laws, data privacy regulations, and platform-specific guidelines.

10. **Performance Benchmarks**: Establish performance benchmarks based on industry standards and competitive analysis. Use these benchmarks to evaluate the effectiveness of your monetisation strategies and set targets for improvement.
11. **Community Engagement**: Engage with your player community throughout the implementation and testing phase. Keep them informed about new features and gather their input. Building a strong relationship with your players can lead to better acceptance of monetisation elements.
12. **Technical Optimization**: Optimize the technical aspects of your monetisation strategies. Ensure that your in-game store, ad servers, and payment gateways are reliable and perform well under different conditions.
13. **Marketing Integration**: Integrate your monetisation strategies with your marketing efforts. Use targeted campaigns to promote in-game purchases, special offers, and subscription plans. Align your marketing messages with the value proposition of your monetisation elements.
14. **Long-Term Monitoring**: After full implementation, continue to monitor the performance of your monetisation strategies. Use real-time analytics to track their impact and make necessary adjustments. Long-term monitoring helps in maintaining the relevance and effectiveness of your strategies.
15. **Player Retention**: Focus on strategies that enhance player retention. Retained players are more likely to spend money in the game. Use retention tactics such as daily rewards, special events, and social features to keep players engaged.

Implementing and testing monetisation strategies is an ongoing process that requires attention to detail, player feedback, and data-driven decision-making. By continuously refining and optimizing these strategies, developers can achieve sustainable revenue growth while maintaining a positive player experience.

19.5 Reviewing and Adapting the Strategy

Reviewing and adapting your monetisation strategy is essential to ensure its continued success and relevance. Here's how to approach this process:

1. **Regular Review Cycles**: Establish regular review cycles to assess the performance of your monetisation strategies. This could be monthly, quarterly, or semi-annually, depending on your game's lifecycle and market dynamics.
2. **Performance Metrics**: Use key performance metrics to evaluate your strategy. Important metrics include ARPU, lifetime value (LTV) of players, conversion rates, retention rates, and player engagement levels. Analyze these metrics to identify strengths and areas for improvement.
3. **Player Feedback**: Continuously collect and analyze player feedback. Use surveys, in-game feedback mechanisms, and social media interactions to understand player sentiments. Address any negative feedback and capitalize on positive responses.
4. **Competitive Analysis**: Regularly analyze your competitors' monetisation strategies. Identify new trends, successful tactics, and potential threats. Use this information to adapt and improve your own strategies.

5. **Market Trends**: Stay informed about market trends and industry developments. The gaming industry is dynamic, with new technologies and player preferences emerging constantly. Adapt your strategies to align with these trends.
6. **Iterative Improvements**: Implement iterative improvements based on your review findings. Make small, incremental changes to your monetisation strategies and test their impact. This approach allows for continuous optimization without significant disruptions.
7. **User Segmentation**: Refine your user segmentation to better target different player groups. Tailor your monetisation strategies to meet the specific needs and preferences of each segment. Personalized experiences can enhance player satisfaction and spending.
8. **A/B Testing**: Continue using A/B testing to evaluate new monetisation ideas. Test different price points, offer structures, and promotional strategies. Use the results to make data-driven decisions and optimize your approach.
9. **Adapting to Feedback**: Be responsive to player feedback. If players express dissatisfaction with certain monetisation elements, address their concerns promptly. This can involve adjusting prices, improving value propositions, or enhancing the overall user experience.
10. **Technical Enhancements**: Regularly update and enhance the technical aspects of your monetisation infrastructure. Ensure that in-game stores, payment systems, and ad networks operate smoothly and efficiently. Technical issues can negatively impact player spending.
11. **Community Engagement**: Maintain active engagement with your player community. Use forums, social media, and in-game events to foster a strong relationship with your players. Engaged communities provide valuable insights and support for your monetisation efforts.
12. **Ethical Considerations**: Continually assess the ethical implications of your monetisation strategies. Avoid practices that exploit players or create negative experiences. Ethical monetisation builds long-term trust and loyalty.
13. **Revenue Diversification**: Explore new revenue streams to diversify your income. This can include expanding into new markets, offering additional virtual goods, or introducing new monetisation models like subscriptions or ad-free options.
14. **Long-Term Planning**: Develop long-term plans for your game's monetisation. Consider how you will sustain revenue over time, especially as the game evolves and the player base matures. Plan for future updates, expansions, and new content to keep players engaged.
15. **Documentation and Learning**: Document the outcomes of your reviews and adaptations. Create a knowledge base of what works and what doesn't. Use this information to guide future monetisation strategies and improve your overall approach.

Reviewing and adapting your monetisation strategy is a continuous process that ensures it remains effective and aligned with player expectations. By staying responsive to feedback, market trends, and performance data, developers can achieve sustainable success in their monetisation efforts.

Chapter 20: Conclusion and Future Directions

20.1 Recap of Key Points

As we conclude this comprehensive guide on mobile game monetisation, it's essential to recap the key points discussed throughout the book:

1. **Understanding the Industry**: The mobile game industry is vast and rapidly evolving. Developers must stay informed about trends, player preferences, and competitive landscapes to create successful monetisation strategies.
2. **Theoretical Foundations**: Economic, psychological, and behavioral theories provide a solid foundation for understanding player spending behavior. These insights help in designing effective monetisation strategies.
3. **Monetisation Models**: Various monetisation models, including free-to-play, premium, freemium, and subscriptions, offer different advantages. Selecting the right model depends on the game type, target audience, and market conditions.
4. **In-Game Purchases**: Designing a balanced in-game economy and offering valuable virtual goods are crucial for successful monetisation. Pricing strategies and case studies of successful games provide practical insights.
5. **Advertising**: Integrating ads in a non-intrusive manner can generate additional revenue. Understanding different ad formats, measuring their effectiveness, and overcoming challenges are key to leveraging in-game advertising.
6. **Player Retention**: Retention strategies, such as gamification, community building, and social features, are vital for sustaining long-term revenue. Engaged players are more likely to spend money in the game.
7. **Monetisation-Friendly Game Design**: Balancing fun and profit, integrating monetisation into the game narrative, and testing mechanics are essential for creating monetisation-friendly game designs.
8. **User Experience**: Ensuring a seamless purchase experience, understanding player personas, and avoiding common UX pitfalls enhance player satisfaction and spending.
9. **Data Analytics**: Data-driven decision-making is critical for optimizing monetisation strategies. Key metrics, tools, and case studies of data-driven strategies provide a roadmap for success.
10. **Legal Considerations**: Navigating the legal landscape, including player privacy, data protection, and consumer protection laws, ensures compliance and builds player trust.
11. **Global Perspectives**: Monetisation strategies must adapt to different markets and cultural preferences. Success stories from various regions highlight the importance of localization.
12. **Emerging Technologies**: AR, VR, blockchain, and AI offer new opportunities for monetisation. Staying ahead of technological advancements can give developers a competitive edge.

13. **Marketing and Monetisation**: Effective marketing strategies, leveraging social media, influencer partnerships, and post-launch marketing are essential for driving player acquisition and revenue.
14. **Case Studies**: Analyzing top-grossing games, learning from their successes and failures, and understanding the evolution of monetisation strategies provide valuable lessons.
15. **Player Feedback**: Collecting, analyzing, and incorporating player feedback into game development builds long-term player loyalty and enhances monetisation efforts.
16. **Indie Developers**: Indie developers face unique challenges in monetisation. Effective strategies, funding, financial planning, and success stories offer guidance for indie game monetisation.
17. **Future Trends**: Predicting market trends, potential disruptors, evolving player expectations, and technological advances help in planning for the future of mobile game monetisation.
18. **Tools and Resources**: Various tools and resources support developers in their monetisation efforts. Continuous learning and community engagement are vital for staying updated and connected.
19. **Building a Strategy**: Developing a monetisation plan, identifying target audiences, creating sustainable models, implementing and testing strategies, and continuously reviewing and adapting them ensure long-term success.

20.2 Reflection on the Evolution of Monetisation

The evolution of monetisation in mobile games reflects the industry's dynamic nature and the constant pursuit of balancing player experience with revenue generation. Here's a reflection on this evolution:

1. **Early Monetisation Models**: The early days of mobile gaming saw straightforward monetisation models, primarily relying on one-time purchases. Games were often sold at a fixed price, with players paying upfront to access the entire game.
2. **Rise of Free-to-Play (F2P)**: The introduction of the free-to-play model revolutionized the industry. Players could download and play games for free, with monetisation occurring through in-game purchases and advertisements. This model significantly expanded the player base and revenue potential.
3. **In-Game Purchases and Microtransactions**: In-game purchases, or microtransactions, became a cornerstone of mobile game monetisation. Players could buy virtual goods, cosmetics, and other enhancements. This model emphasized player choice and personalization.
4. **Subscription Models**: Subscription models emerged as another viable monetisation strategy. Offering players access to exclusive content, features, or benefits for a recurring fee provided a steady revenue stream. This model is particularly effective for games with ongoing updates and content.
5. **Ad Integration**: Advertising became an integral part of monetisation strategies. Rewarded videos, interstitials, and banner ads offered additional revenue without directly charging players. The challenge has been to integrate ads in a way that does not disrupt the gaming experience.

6. **Hybrid Models**: Many games adopted hybrid monetisation models, combining elements of free-to-play, in-game purchases, and subscriptions. This approach allows for diversified revenue streams and caters to different player preferences.
7. **Ethical Considerations**: As monetisation strategies evolved, ethical considerations became increasingly important. Developers had to balance revenue generation with fair and transparent practices to avoid exploiting players. Ethical monetisation fosters long-term trust and loyalty.
8. **Technological Advancements**: Technological advancements, such as AR, VR, blockchain, and AI, have opened new avenues for monetisation. These technologies enable innovative gameplay experiences and novel ways to engage and monetize players.
9. **Data-Driven Approaches**: The use of data analytics transformed monetisation strategies. Developers could now track player behavior, spending patterns, and engagement levels to make informed decisions. This data-driven approach allows for continuous optimization and personalization.
10. **Globalization**: The global reach of mobile games necessitated the adaptation of monetisation strategies to different markets. Cultural differences, economic conditions, and player preferences influenced how games were monetized in various regions.
11. **Community and Social Features**: Building strong player communities and integrating social features became essential for monetisation. Engaged communities provided valuable feedback and supported long-term revenue through loyalty and social interactions.
12. **Regulatory Landscape**: The evolving regulatory landscape required developers to stay compliant with laws and regulations. Issues such as data privacy, consumer protection, and advertising standards became critical considerations.
13. **Future Directions**: Looking ahead, the future of mobile game monetisation will likely involve more personalized and immersive experiences. Advances in technology, player expectations, and market dynamics will continue to shape monetisation strategies.

Reflecting on the evolution of monetisation in mobile games highlights the industry's adaptability and innovation. Developers have continually refined their strategies to enhance player experiences while achieving sustainable revenue growth.

20.3 Challenges and Opportunities Ahead

The mobile game industry faces several challenges and opportunities as it continues to evolve. Here are some of the key aspects to consider:

Challenges

1. **Market Saturation**: The mobile game market is highly saturated, with thousands of new games released each year. Standing out and attracting players in such a competitive environment is increasingly difficult.

2. **Player Retention**: Retaining players over the long term remains a significant challenge. With numerous gaming options available, keeping players engaged and coming back to the game requires continuous effort and innovation.
3. **Monetisation Balance**: Finding the right balance between monetisation and player experience is crucial. Overly aggressive monetisation tactics can lead to player frustration and churn, while under-monetisation can impact revenue.
4. **Regulatory Compliance**: Navigating the complex regulatory landscape, including data privacy laws, consumer protection regulations, and advertising standards, requires constant vigilance and adaptation.
5. **Technological Advancements**: Keeping up with rapid technological advancements and integrating new technologies like AR, VR, blockchain, and AI into games can be resource-intensive and challenging.
6. **Ethical Concerns**: Ethical considerations in monetisation practices are increasingly important. Developers must ensure that their strategies are fair, transparent, and do not exploit players.
7. **Ad Blocking**: The rise of ad-blocking technologies poses a challenge for games that rely on advertising revenue. Developers need to find ways to offer value through ads that players are willing to engage with.
8. **Cultural Differences**: Monetisation strategies that work well in one region may not be effective in another. Adapting to cultural differences and player preferences across global markets requires a nuanced approach.

Opportunities

1. **Emerging Markets**: Expanding into emerging markets presents significant growth opportunities. These markets often have untapped player bases and growing smartphone adoption rates.
2. **Cross-Platform Play**: Enabling cross-platform play can enhance player engagement and monetisation. Players can continue their gaming experience across different devices, increasing retention and spending.
3. **Subscription Services**: Subscription models offer a steady revenue stream and can be particularly effective for games with ongoing content updates and exclusive features.
4. **Personalization**: Advances in data analytics and AI enable personalized gaming experiences. Tailoring content, offers, and recommendations to individual players can enhance engagement and monetisation.
5. **Social and Community Features**: Building strong player communities and integrating social features can drive long-term engagement and monetisation. Social interactions and community events create a sense of belonging and loyalty.
6. **Innovative Monetisation Models**: Exploring new and innovative monetisation models can open up additional revenue streams. This includes integrating blockchain for unique virtual goods or leveraging AR for immersive ad experiences.
7. **Player Feedback Integration**: Actively involving players in the development process through feedback and beta testing can lead to better monetisation strategies. Players who feel heard are more likely to support the game financially.
8. **Ethical Monetisation**: Emphasizing ethical monetisation practices can build long-term trust and loyalty. Players are more likely to support games that treat them fairly and offer real value for their money.

9. **Collaborations and Partnerships**: Partnering with other companies, brands, or influencers can enhance monetisation efforts. Collaborations can introduce new audiences to the game and offer unique promotional opportunities.
10. **Continuous Innovation**: The mobile game industry thrives on innovation. Continuously exploring new ideas, gameplay mechanics, and monetisation strategies can keep the game fresh and engaging for players.

The challenges and opportunities ahead require developers to stay agile, innovative, and responsive to player needs and market trends. By addressing challenges proactively and seizing opportunities, developers can achieve sustainable success in the evolving mobile game industry.

20.4 Final Thoughts on Ethical Monetisation

Ethical monetisation is crucial for the long-term success and sustainability of mobile games. Here are some final thoughts on how developers can achieve ethical monetisation:

1. **Player-Centric Approach**: Place players at the center of your monetisation strategy. Understand their needs, preferences, and pain points. Design monetisation elements that enhance their gaming experience rather than detracting from it.
2. **Transparent Pricing**: Ensure that pricing for in-game purchases is clear and transparent. Players should understand what they are paying for and what value they are receiving. Avoid hidden costs or deceptive practices.
3. **Fair Value Proposition**: Offer fair value for money. In-game purchases should provide real benefits and enhance the gameplay experience. Avoid overpriced items or pay-to-win mechanics that create an unfair advantage.
4. **Avoid Exploitation**: Refrain from exploiting players through manipulative tactics. This includes avoiding predatory practices such as loot boxes with low odds, excessive paywalls, or pressure tactics to make players spend money.
5. **Balanced Gameplay**: Maintain a balance between free and paid content. Free players should still enjoy the game, while paying players receive additional benefits that do not disrupt the overall balance of the game.
6. **Rewarding Loyalty**: Reward loyal players with meaningful incentives. This can include exclusive content, special events, or loyalty programs. Recognizing and rewarding player loyalty fosters a positive relationship.
7. **Community Engagement**: Engage with your player community and listen to their feedback. Actively involve players in the development process and be responsive to their concerns and suggestions.
8. **Data Privacy**: Protect player data and ensure compliance with data privacy regulations. Be transparent about data collection practices and give players control over their personal information.
9. **Ethical Advertising**: Integrate ads in a way that does not disrupt the gameplay experience. Use ad formats that offer value to players, such as rewarded videos, and avoid excessive or intrusive ads.
10. **Sustainable Practices**: Focus on long-term sustainability rather than short-term gains. Building a loyal player base through ethical practices leads to sustained revenue and positive word-of-mouth.

11. **Regulatory Compliance**: Stay informed about and comply with relevant regulations and industry standards. This includes consumer protection laws, advertising standards, and platform-specific guidelines.
12. **Continuous Improvement**: Continuously evaluate and improve your monetisation practices. Use player feedback, data analytics, and industry trends to refine your strategies and ensure they remain ethical and effective.
13. **Transparency in Updates**: When updating the game, be transparent about changes to monetisation elements. Clearly communicate any adjustments to pricing, in-game economies, or purchase options.
14. **Fair Play**: Ensure that your game promotes fair play. Avoid mechanics that give paying players an unfair advantage over non-paying players. Strive to create a level playing field where skill and strategy are rewarded.
15. **Positive Impact**: Aim to have a positive impact on the gaming community. Support initiatives that promote healthy gaming habits, inclusivity, and social responsibility.

Ethical monetisation is not just about generating revenue; it's about building trust, loyalty, and a positive relationship with your players. By prioritizing ethics in your monetisation strategy, you can achieve long-term success and create a game that players love and support.

20.5 Call to Action for Game Developers

As we conclude this guide, it's time to put these insights into action. Here's a call to action for game developers to create successful and ethical monetisation strategies:

1. **Commit to Learning**: Continuously educate yourself about the latest trends, technologies, and best practices in mobile game monetisation. Stay curious and open to new ideas.
2. **Understand Your Players**: Invest time in understanding your player base. Develop detailed player personas, gather feedback, and engage with your community to tailor your monetisation strategies to their needs.
3. **Experiment and Innovate**: Don't be afraid to experiment with different monetisation models and strategies. Use A/B testing to find what works best and be innovative in your approach.
4. **Prioritize Ethics**: Make ethical considerations a cornerstone of your monetisation strategy. Ensure that your practices are fair, transparent, and respectful of your players.
5. **Leverage Data**: Use data analytics to inform your decisions. Track key performance metrics, analyze player behavior, and use insights to optimize your monetisation strategies.
6. **Stay Compliant**: Keep abreast of legal and regulatory requirements. Ensure that your monetisation practices comply with relevant laws and industry standards to build trust with your players.
7. **Engage with Your Community**: Build and maintain a strong player community. Engage with your players through social media, forums, and in-game events. Listen to their feedback and incorporate it into your game development.

8. **Focus on Retention**: Implement strategies that enhance player retention. Use gamification, social features, and regular content updates to keep players engaged and coming back.
9. **Balance Fun and Profit**: Strive to create a balance between generating revenue and providing an enjoyable gaming experience. Avoid aggressive monetisation tactics that can detract from the fun.
10. **Document and Share**: Document your monetisation strategies, successes, and lessons learned. Share your experiences with the developer community to contribute to collective knowledge and improvement.
11. **Plan for the Future**: Develop a long-term vision for your game's monetisation. Plan for future updates, expansions, and new content to sustain player interest and revenue.
12. **Stay Adaptable**: Be prepared to adapt your strategies based on market trends, player feedback, and technological advancements. Flexibility and responsiveness are key to long-term success.
13. **Collaborate**: Collaborate with other developers, brands, and influencers. Partnerships can introduce new audiences to your game and offer unique promotional opportunities.
14. **Focus on Quality**: Ensure that your game is high quality, with engaging gameplay and a seamless user experience. A great game is the foundation of successful monetisation.
15. **Take Action**: Finally, take action. Implement the strategies discussed in this guide, monitor their performance, and continuously refine your approach. Success in mobile game monetisation requires dedication, creativity, and a player-first mindset.

By taking these steps, game developers can create monetisation strategies that are not only profitable but also ethical and player-centric. The future of mobile game monetisation is bright for those who prioritize innovation, ethics, and a deep understanding of their players.

www.ingramcontent.com/pod-product-compliance
Lightning Source LLC
Chambersburg PA
CBHW071921210526
45479CB00002B/506